Lessons from God

by Carla Cameron

Innovo
Publishing

Published by
Innovo Publishing, LLC
www.innovopublishing.com
1-888-546-2111

Providing Full-Service Publishing Services for
Christian Organizations & Authors: Hardbacks, Paperbacks,
eBooks, Audio Books, & iPhone Application Books

LESSONS FROM GOD
Copyright © 2010 by Carla Cameron
All rights reserved.

ISBN 13: 978-1-936076-24-6
ISBN 10: 1-936076-24-1

Cover Design & Interior Layout: Innovo Publishing, LLC

Printed in the United States of America
U.S. Printing History
Second Edition: July 2010

Dedicated to my mother,
Mary Dillon (1946-1998)

Mom, I love you and thank you for always believing in me and in this book. I miss you and I look forward to one of your huge hugs when I get to heaven.

ACKNOWLEDGMENTS

I would like to thank God
for taking the time to speak to my heart.
For bringing healing, correction, direction and
understanding to my life.

I would also like to thank all the people
who have helped judge, proof and assemble these lessons,
especially my husband Tim and good friend Joyce Parker.

I pray that as you read this book,
you will be richly blessed with a deeper
understanding and relationship with God.

Carla Cameron

INTRODUCTION

I cannot think of a better way to start *Lessons from God* than from a timeless lesson in Proverbs. For years I have known that Proverbs 3:5-6 was my life scripture, but until this year I had never read the whole Proverb. I really had missed out on knowing and embracing more incredible truth. Take a moment to read Proverbs 3. I think you will see that God sums up how we are to live our lives and what we can expect from Him if we will trust, seek, and obey.

Proverbs 3:1-31

My son, do not forget my teaching, but let your heart keep my commandments, for length of days and years of life and peace they will add to you.

Let not steadfast love and faithfulness forsake you; bind them around your neck; write them on the tablet of your heart.
So you will find favor and good success in the sight of God and man.
*Trust in the LORD with all your heart, and do not lean on your own understanding. In all your ways acknowledge Him, and He will make straight your paths.
Be not wise in your own eyes; fear the LORD, and turn away from evil. It will be healing to your flesh and refreshment to your bones.
Honor the LORD with your wealth and with the firstfruits of all your produce; then your barns will be filled with plenty, and your vats will be bursting with wine.
My son, do not despise the LORD's discipline or be weary of His reproof, for the LORD reproves him whom He loves, as a father the son in whom he delights.
Blessed is the one who finds wisdom, and the one who gets understanding, for the gain from her is better than gain from silver and her profit better than gold.

She is more precious than jewels, and nothing you desire can compare with her. Long life is in her right hand; in her left hand are riches and honor.

Her ways are ways of pleasantness, and all her paths are peace. She is a tree of life to those who lay hold of her; those who hold her fast are called blessed.

The LORD by wisdom founded the earth; by understanding He established the heavens; by His knowledge the deeps broke open, and the clouds drop down the dew.

My son, do not lose sight of these-- keep sound wisdom and discretion, and they will be life for your soul and adornment for your neck.

Then you will walk on your way securely, and your foot will not stumble. If you lie down, you will not be afraid; when you lie down, your sleep will be sweet.

Do not be afraid of sudden terror or of the ruin of the wicked, when it comes, for the LORD will be your confidence and will keep your foot from being caught.

Do not withhold good from those to whom it is due, when it is in your power to do it.

Do not say to your neighbor, "Go, and come again, tomorrow I will give it"--when you have it with you.

Do not plan evil against your neighbor, who dwells trustingly beside you.

Do not contend with a man for no reason, when he has done you no harm.

Do not envy a man of violence and do not choose any of his ways, for the devious person is an abomination to the LORD, but the upright are in His confidence.

The LORD's curse is on the house of the wicked, but He blesses the dwelling of the righteous. Toward the scorners He is scornful, but to the humble He gives favor. The wise will inherit honor, but fools get disgrace.

THE PRICELESS TREASURE

The Bible is like a priceless treasure waiting to be found.

Some find it
but never to open it.

Others open it
but don't know what the treasure is.

Blessed are those who realize that the treasure is
in the freedom their heart has when it begins
to comprehend God's love.

The truly blessed are those
who realize the priceless treasure is a living God
and not just a page of the Bible!
cc

TABLE OF CONTENTS

Volume I

*Y*OUR *H*EART

Let Me have your whole heart,
so I can mend its brokenness.

I don't just want to restore it; I want to make it new.

Please trust Me with your heart, as I have been healing and
purifying hearts since the beginning of time.

I know what pleases My heart and if you'll let Me build your
life on what pleases Me, you shall be truly blessed.

Every promise I have ever made
throughout history will come to pass.
This includes the promises I have made to you.

There will be many times,
I will call upon you to help minister to My people.

Will you speak from your wisdom, or from Mine?
Always trust Me for the words to say.

It will be My pleasure to give you opportunities
to share with My children, the love I've shared with you.
But first let Me love you.
Let Me wrap My arms of love and comfort around you.

Let Me hold you until every fear
you have ever felt has been replaced by
My unconditional love.
cc

1 John 4:18

There is no fear in love; but perfect love casts out fear: because
fear hath torment. He that fears is not made perfect in love.

LISTEN

*You cannot serve Me unless you listen to what I would have
you to do. Stop blocking out My voice.*

What are you afraid of?

*Do you think I Am a scary God?
Ask yourself this question. Give Me your fears.*

*Allow Me to show you the truth. I'm a gentle, loving God who
desires to communicate with My children.*

Please let Me in on a daily basis.

*How can you go all day without hearing Me?
Doesn't that disturb you? If it does, then why don't you lend
Me your spiritual ears and listen to all the ways
I speak to you throughout the day.*

When your mind is calm your heart can hear.

*My sheep hear My voice... (John 10:27)
Start believing that I want to speak with you.*

*Don't limit My approach to you.
Stop doubting and start listening.
Let Me be free to express Myself to you and others.*

*Who do you think you need to be?
What are you waiting for?
Do I have to send down an angel
before you realize that I wish to speak to you?*

*Let Me be to you as the sun is to the flower.
The flower sits for hours in the warmth of the sun,
without the need to say a word, just absorbing the life giving
presence of the sun.*

My child, sit before Me as the flower does.
Let My words bring life into your soul.
All of My flowers are precious to Me.
Each one with a different color and fragrance;
each one knowing I'm God and will bathe them with the sun
and awaken them with the softness of My dew.

Oh, My child, how much more do I love thee,
please open up to Me.

I Am continually with you; won't you join in My company?

Let My thoughts caress your mind.
Let My stillness surround your body
so that you may be free to be still before Me.

Stop listening to this worlds doubt. Get to know My heart and
what I would say about your life. You have let people's doubt
blow out your light of hope in Me too easily. Guard your
heart and the beliefs you put into it.

Come to Me, the Creator of the Universe.
I know your heart and the struggles you face, better than
anyone. I can, with all tenderness,
lead you to the right decision.

Seek My counsel and I will share My wisdom with you.
Let Me protect you from the harm of a wrong decision.
A decision that would take you down a path that leads you
away from My perfect will for your life. (Proverbs 2:1-12)

Take joy, My child, for I'm God.
I Am forever watching over you. (Psalms 91:11)
cc

Confusion

Do not allow your mind to be filled with man's theories.
Rely on Me for the answers you seek.

Do not let doubt and fear be your teachers.

Do not let the circumstances of your life bring you confusion.
Come to Me. Allow Me to share with you the lessons
I wish to teach you from it.

My child, I see how the choices of this world have tossed you
about. Do not let feelings and frustrations come between you
and I. (James 1:5-6)

When you start to feel overwhelmed,
come to Me and tell Me of your troubles.
Let My words of wisdom give you the truth
that will break you free from your mind's bondage.

Please allow My truth, not man's, to guard your mind.

Confusion starts when you do not know or understand My
perfect will; it's fueled from doubt and fear which is bred into
your life through man's beliefs and satan's lies.

You must stop pondering the lies of your enemies.

Satan and man can only lie to you, they can't make you
believe it. They can try to convince you,
but you don't have to believe.

I Am not the author of confusion, but of a sound mind.
(1 Corinthians 14:33) (2 Timothy 1:7)

I have given you authority over satan and his troops.
Stop allowing him to boss you around.
I want you to be able to recognize the difference between his
voice and Mine. (Luke 10:19)

I speak to you out of truth and love,
he speaks to you out of lies and condemnation.
Condemnation is a tool for satan's use, not Mine

The only power satan has over you is the power you let him
have, in your actions and thought life.

Only the Scriptures that have reached your heart can guard
your mind from false knowledge.
(Psalms 37:31 and 119) (Proverbs 2:10-12)

You must be able to recognize the lies of the enemy at the
moment they are being spoken or he will not flee from you.
(James 4:7) (Ephesians 6:10-18)

The only way to do this is to rely on My Holy Spirit,
not yourself, to guide you into all truth.

Take inventory of what you have been thinking...
Ask yourself;
Why am I confused?
What am I afraid of?
Why am I doubting?

What does the Bible say about my situation?
What was the lie of doubt I started to believe?
Then hand that lie to Me so I can teach you My truth,
which will set you free.

You must learn to take every thought captive.
(2 Corinthian 10:5)

When you are waiting on Me do not become impatient,
and turn to the world for answers that only I have.
Instead have faith. Trust Me with the outcome.

I do not want you to live by doubt
but by faith in Me and My promises.
Faith means believing in Me no matter what the
circumstances look like.

17

Man's spoken disbeliefs in Me are the lies that will steal your peace and destroy your faith in Me.
If you listen, they will rob you of the many promises and desires I have given you.

Satan will use anyone or anything he can;
to tell you lies about your future (don't listen)
to remind you of your past mistakes (you're forgiven)
to come between us (don't let him).

Don't let anyone rob you of My peace and presence.
Do not keep a conversation with those
who condemn you or Me.

I Am the Giver of all you need, but you must believe this truth.
(Philippians 4:19-20)

Do not look to the world for your supply. Let Me give to you
out of My riches and glory.

Listen to Me always, and not the doubt of your enemies.
I will always make the way possible,
if I have called you in a certain direction.

As I did with Moses, I can part any sea
of confusion and fear. Learn to trust Me completely,
I will not play tricks on you.

I LOVE YOU

You are so valuable to Me and My kingdom.
Don't let anyone else convince you otherwise.

Do not let anyone tell you I have forgotten you or your
prayers. I have heard each one of My children's cries.

I have promised to be your God....
Are you willing to let Me?
cc

MY LOVE FOR YOU

I communicate My love to you in so many ways.
Learn to recognize My love.

Each bird you hear
is an orchestrated love song prepared
just for your hearing.

Each breeze you feel is a refreshing touch for your soul.

Let each friend's hug bring you comfort and love,
for it is My arms holding you.

Take time to smell a beautiful flower
and know that the trust in your prayers
smell that good to Me.

When the world has gotten you down,
turn to Me for the joy you so desperately need.
I created life for joy, not sorrow.

Praise Me for the many things I have created.

Let laughter run from your mouth. Each ear that hears will
know that such joy can only be found
in union with Me.

Don't let the busyness of a day rob you of the many blessings I
want to share with you.

When you recognize My love as a blessing,
your appreciation releases
My joy and pleasure in giving you more.

Oh My child, please fill up your soul with My love,
so you can tell others of My great love for them.

Only when you recognize and realize My unending love,
can you share with them, My complete love.
My love has no limits,
no expectations, only desires for My people.

I desire for My people to know who I Am.
To know the greatest love they can receive
is the sacrifice of My Son's life.

Each time you think of Jesus,
remember that without the sacrifice of His life,
no one could be washed clean of their sins.

Jesus was My Love made flesh,
to become a sacrifice so that all
who wanted to be forever with Me, could.

Please tell others of the love I gave in Jesus.
(Mark 16:15-16)

Give My lost the truth and a chance to accept the gift of My
Son. It is through My Son, that the power of satan was
broken. Jesus' life is the only sacrifice
that can cover My people from their sins.
(John 3:16) (Ephesians 2:8)

Without this acceptance of My Son,
no one, no matter how holy he lives his life,
can enter My gates of Heaven.
(John 14:6)

Remember most of all, that I love you,
and because of My Son's love for you too,
you have the choice of an eternity with Me and My Son
or eternal death in hell.
(Romans 6:23)
cc

WHAT IS YOUR MIND THINKING?

*You must be able to stop your mind from wandering away
from Me. At any moment, you should be able to hear Me over
the rumblings of your own thoughts.*

*Rid your mind of all its worries and concern. Hand each one
to Me, until nothing else commands your attention.*

*Practice this daily, hourly until it is habit. Soon, your mind
will honor Me throughout the day. (Mark 12:30)*

I long for you to give Me the attention your thoughts get.

*Let Me open your spiritual ears.
Let Me fill your mind with My thoughts.*

*I have so much to share with you. Please let go of your world
of thoughts and enter into daily life with Me.*

*My heart longs for intimate communion with My people.
I want to kiss their thoughts each morning
with My inspiration.*

*Help My people understand
how much I long to be God in their lives.*

*Help them to realize there is not one day that goes by
that I Am not trying to break down
the walls of their minds.*

*They see Me as a cold, distant God.
They come to Me only when they need something.*

I want to be a part of their daily lives.

I know their lives are busy.

But too busy, for their Creator,
the One who designed their very being?

I Am so tired of left-over's.
I Am starving for My people to allow Me,
My rightful place in their lives.

I want them to come to Me,
and share their thoughts and desires, whether good or bad.

So many days go by without even a word from some.
My heart longs for them to hear and respond to My voice.

I long to lead My people out of the bondage
this world has put them in.

When will they realize I love them each day?
That I long to be with them for more
than just one or two days a week.

Are My requests too difficult? Then ask Me for help.
(Hebrews 8:10-12)

Is loving Me throughout the day too much of a task?
(Matthew 22:37)

Do My people not enjoy My presence?

Do not forget that I Am speaking to you, too.

I need My people to believe in Me.
They put so much trust in this world and not in Me.

How long do I have to wait before I Am honored as God?

I have been so loving and patient with My people.
Yet most think when the storm hits that I have left them.
This grieves My heart so.

*For centuries My people have chosen their own lifestyle,
instead of Mine. Have I not laid out in black and white print,
My guidelines for a peaceful life?*

*Apostle Paul knew no physical peace and yet he had inner
peace; the kind I desire for all My children.
Come to Me for this peace, not your world.*

*Listen well to My Words for I will hold you accountable,
because now you know what truly breaks My heart.*

*Please allow Me to come into your world.
Allow My strength and promises to calm
your wind blown mind.*

*I do truly love you.
I wait each morning for you to awake
and share your day with Me.*
cc

Philippians 4:4-8

Rejoice in the Lord always; again I will say, Rejoice. Let your reasonableness be known to everyone. The Lord is at hand; do not be anxious about anything, but in everything by prayer and supplication with thanksgiving let your requests be made known to God.

And the peace of God, which surpasses all understanding, will guard your hearts and your minds in Christ Jesus.

Finally, brothers, whatever is true, whatever is honorable, whatever is just, whatever is pure, whatever is lovely, whatever is commendable, if there is any excellence, if there is anything worthy of praise, think about these things.

PLEASE WAIT FOR MY BEST

You are so precious to Me, why can't you rest in this truth?

You keep searching for Me through people.
When are you going to realize
I Am the one to feed you, not man?

It is good to have fellowship,
but not if you are living off what they give you.
I want you to be well fed by Me
so that you might share your feast with others.

I have so many things for you to do. When can I trust you not
to run off with your duties and skip the many meals I have
prepared for you?

You must let Me be a part of each activity, because I know
exactly how it should be done and you don't.
Please don't run off and stop listening to My direction.
Because when you do, you use your abilities and not Mine.
(Psalms 32:8-9)

Only I know the perfect path
to complete all that I have assigned you to do.
When I give you a task; I know I can fulfill it through you.

There will be many times that I will give you a task that is
beyond your present capabilities. Do not wear yourself out
trying to complete it without Me.

I must have your trust and willingness
to do all that I have asked, when I ask it.

When I give you a burning desire or vision,
give it back to Me so that I can fulfill it...

Please don't wallow in disbelief
and try to figure out if it's possible or not.

I know it's possible or I would not have given it to you.

I want you to have vision... not your own, but Mine.

Trust Me with the desires I give you, knowing that I have the ability to work out all the details.

You must let go of the fears you hold inside and realize that it is through your weakness that others can see Me and the great things I Am doing through you.

Only when you truly become an open vessel, can I pour into you the necessary ingredients to make the vision possible. More than being an open vessel, you must be a yielding one.

This means that when you see a great opportunity, turn to Me and ask if it is the one I want you to take.

You must not busy yourself with good opportunities. Know that if it is from Me, it will be the very best. You must rest in this.

Wait for Me to move and watch for My leading. Don't settle for second best; allow Me to give you My best. Sometimes that comes from waiting and letting great opportunities pass you by.

You must be certain it is I leading you, not your own agenda.

Anything you do that is outside of what I have called you to do is not glorifying to Me but an act of disobedience.

Learn to listen and trust My voice. Be willing to do nothing, if that is what I want you to do. I love you and I have missed you....
cc

TRUST ME

Again, I tell you how precious you are to Me.
You must realize this, before we can run and play together.

My love for you is endless; it knows no time.

I want all you do for Me to come out of this love. I want you
to have much joy in the life I have chosen for you.

Yes, there will be trials and troubles, but learn to trust and
turn to Me in each one. At no moment have I forgotten you or
the situation you are faced with.

Yes, some of the turmoil in your life has been from wrong
choices you have made. I will pick you up and carry you if
necessary, to get you back to the place of My choosing.

Do not fear past mistakes, learn from them.

You need but just ask and I will close the door to your
mistakes, never to be reopened again. (Hebrews 10:17)

I do not want you to live with pain or regret.
I Am the Forgiver and Healer.
(1 Peter 2:24)

You must be willing to let Me have the key
to your heart, so I can unlock your past.
Let Me enter in and remove
what is not necessary for your growth.
Will you trust Me with your hurting heart?

You may not have realized it,
but My heart ached each time yours did.
How I wanted you to run to Me for comfort; but instead,
both our hearts stayed broken.

It is time for you to walk with a newness of Spirit.
One that recognizes My comfort and love.

My Spirit will help and instruct you in the ways you should
go, if you will listen and obey My voice.
(Psalms 32:8)

Please realize that I do all things through love
and for the glory of My Kingdom.

Come and share with Me your life.
Let Me roam freely into your thoughts and into your heart.
Let Me help you complete the work
that I assigned to you at conception.

Allow Me to guide and nurture you through the storms of life.
Let Me be the umbrella and raincoat
that is needed to play out in the rain.

I want you to share in My joy and warmth.
You are never alone, I Am always one thought away.

I LOVE YOU!!!
Remember this, when you are feeling overwhelmed.

Call on Me first and not your friend; I will always be waiting
and never let you down.

Trust My timing and not the world's.

When the sprinkle has turned into a flood,
I Am there holding you afloat. I will not let you drown.

When My peace is not felt,
it's because you have not let Me share it with you.

Don't be afraid to trust Me.
cc

My Living Truth

*I created the Bible to give you
truth, freedom, hope and understanding of Who I Am.*

*Please don't ever think Scripture is not important.
I have so many secrets and promises I want to share with
you. So many crucial lessons you will learn from
My children's mistakes. (1 Corinthians 2:9)*

If you would only pick up your Bible and read it more.

*I breathed life into the Bible so that it could be an inspiration
to those who read it. My words live forever.*

*As you read about Me, I become more alive to you.
It allows you to see tangible proof of
My presence and power.*

*Each time you pick up the Bible,
invite Me to read it with you so I can teach you
the value and true meaning of the words written down.
(John 14:26)*

*You need to be well aware of what My truths are so
when satan comes to test you, you can defeat him with truth.
(Ephesians 6:11-18)*

*Not only must you learn the truth,
you must accept and apply it.*

*I will not abandon you, but I do want you to be able to stand
when you don't feel My presence.
My truth helps you stand.*

You must stand on My Word so when satan comes to steal away a promise or to tell you a lie, you will know what I have to say about the given subject.
You must claim the truth of what is rightfully yours. Stop allowing satan to trick you out of the many blessings and privileges a relationship with Me provides.

Continually seek to hear My voice.
Don't give up until you have broken through the walls of worry, doubt and fear. (2 Corinthians 10:5)

Allow My thoughts to penetrate your current surroundings. I Am always waiting for you to enter My presence. (Hebrew 4:16)

I Am not withholding from you.
It is your present state of mind that is blocking Me out.
Learn to open up to Me during all times of the day.
cc

Hebrews 4:16

(KJVR) "Let us therefore come boldly unto the throne of grace, that we may obtain mercy, and find grace to help in time of need."

John 8:31-32

So Jesus said to those who believed in him, "If you obey My teaching, you are really My disciples; you will know the truth, and the truth will set you free."

Come To Me

My precious Child,

I do not want acts of service, I want obedience.

*All the work in the world will not please Me
if I haven't told you to do it... (1 Samuel 15:22)*

*You must come to a place where I alone Am the one speaking
to you. (You rely too much on others and not ME.) Please
stop fooling yourself into believing that this kind of fellowship
is pleasing to Me.*

What can they give you that I can not?

*If you need a tangible feeling, then wait before Me,
believing that I will come to you and
you will feel My presence.*

*As long as you are seeking from man what only I can give,
you will never be satisfied. Stop searching in the world for
what is rightfully yours when you come into My presence.*

Is it scary to wait upon Me? What are you afraid of?

*Are you afraid you have disappointed Me,
and I will withhold My presence?*

*My child, there is nothing you can do to separate My love
from you. All the sin in the world cannot separate us.*

*My Son died for that sin so that you could come to Me with all
of your burdens. (Romans 8:35-39)*

*There is not one thing that goes on in your daily life,
whether big or small, that I don't want to be a part of.*

*Allow My Holy Spirit to be your Guide, Best Friend and
Comforter. Come to Me instead of others,
so I can be these things to you. (Galatians 5:18)*

*Do not hide from Me when you have been disobedient,
instead come to Me and ask
for My strength and forgiveness.*

*How Am I supposed to comfort you?
When you think I don't care?
When you think I don't understand?
When you think I won't forgive you?*
cc

John 14:16-21 (KJVR)

And I will pray to the Father, and he shall give you another
Comforter, that He may abide with you forever; Even the Spirit
of truth; whom the world cannot receive, because it seeth Him
not, neither knoweth Him: but ye know Him; for He dwelleth
with you, and shall be in you.

I will not leave you comfortless: I will come to you. Yet a little
while, and the world seeth Me no more; but ye see Me: because
I live, ye shall live also.

At that day ye shall know that I am in My Father, and ye in Me,
and I in you. He that hath My commandments, and keepeth
them, he it is that loveth Me: and he that loveth Me shall be
loved of My Father, and I will love him, and will manifest
Myself to him.

PERSECUTION

*Satan uses people close to you to persecute you and get you
off track.   You may not see Me in it at all, but this is still
persecution for My sake.*

*When satan sees you prospering My Kingdom and taking
from his; he will do anything in his power to stop you.
He will use anyone or anything to bring you doubt and
temptations.*

*He has no authority over you unless you give it to him.
You are the one who has been given authority
over all the power of the enemy. (Luke 10:19)*

*Satan will try to speak lies to your mind.
You must not listen!! He gains access in your life through
doors of doubt and temptations. The only way to close these
doors is with My truth and strength living in you.*

*He will try to get you to believe that I have forgotten you and
stopped loving you, because of the turmoil in your life.*

*You must believe I Am always with you,
even when you disobey Me.
My love and commitment to you, was sealed on the cross.*

*I will never stop loving you as I have made a promise...
I will never leave you nor forget about you.
You must remove all doubt and know
that I Am forever with you. (Joshua 1:5-9)*

*Satan's greatest strategy is
to get you to doubt My love for you.
No matter what the circumstances look like. No matter how
many people are against you. I Am there.
(Romans 8:38)*

cc

Volume II

I AM CALLING YOU OUT

I Am calling you out My child, to go to My children:

Who don't have ears to hear Me.
Who don't have hearts to love Me.
Who haven't seen My Glory.
Who haven't tasted My goodness.
Who haven't felt My loving arms.

*I Am calling you out of this world's bondage so that you can
share with others My love which will set them free.*

*But I caution you child, let the results lie in My hands.
Do not take on the burden of the results. Leave that to Me.*

Do all I ask of you and this will please Me.

*Do not count souls as your victories,
because they are Mine. Count your times of obedience;
as this will bring you great joy.
Do not let satan tell you that you are not victorious because
you do not see the results.*

*Know that in your obedience to Me and My Words,
you will always be victorious.
Do not give up when you are disobedient.*

*Give to Me your sorrow and regret.
I will mend your life stronger than before.   (1Peter 5:8-10)*

No act of disobedience can stop My love for you.

*Know that when you fall, I Am reaching down to pick you up.
I will not let any sin or anyone keep you down,
if you will but reach for My hand with a repentant heart.
(1 John 1:9)*
cc

PERFECTION

*My child, don't be afraid of what people will say as you come
closer to Me. People will not understand the sacrifices you
will make for Me. Please don't listen to their opinions.*

*Listen to the cry of My heart as it calls you closer.
Do not listen to the fear you may still have in your heart.
I will always love you unconditionally, and will never leave you.*

*Nothing I do is by accident or by chance.
(Ecclesiastes 3:1-15)*

*I Am your God. I Am here to protect you and I would not let
anything hurt you unless I had a use for your pain.
(1 Peter 4:12-19)*

*Are you willing to trust Me?
You need to trust Me above all else.*

*In the hour of your toughest testing,
I Am there showing you the way I desire you to go.
(1 Corinthians 10:13)*

You are as a precious stone to Me.   (1 Peter 2:1-10)

*Please let Me cut away the parts of your life
that inhibit My beauty and purity
from shining through you.*

*Please allow Me to polish you to perfection.
This is done by being tested and tried
so that you can see what truly is in your heart.*

*Perfection is not what you can do for Me.
Perfection is your heart being completely free
to listen and obey My voice.*

Oh, My child, you need to listen to Me.
So many times you have blocked out My voice
by listening to the voice of others.

Don't be afraid, I have the ability to comfort you,
if you would just turn to Me and listen completely.

I will not say things to hurt you,
but I do need to correct and direct your footsteps.
Open up your heart and ears to Me and listen completely.
Don't block Me out when you're afraid of what I will say.

I Am the strength and love you need.
I Am the Giver of all that is good.

So come to Me and receive all that I have for you.
Let My words of life which are My living waters
wash you to perfection.
cc

1 Peter 4:12-19

My dear friends, do not be surprised at the painful test you are suffering, as though something unusual were happening to you. Rather be glad that you are sharing Christ's sufferings, so that you may be full of joy when his glory is revealed.

Happy are you if you are insulted because you are Christ's followers; this means that the glorious Spirit, the Spirit of God, is resting on you.

If you suffer, it must not be because you are a murderer or a thief or a criminal or a meddler in other people's affairs. However, if you suffer because you are a Christian, don't be ashamed of it, but thank God that you bear Christ's name.

So then, those who suffer because it is God's will for them, should by their good actions trust themselves completely to their Creator, who always keeps his promise.

I NEED ALL MY WORKERS

*If I did not have plans for you here on earth,
I would have already taken you home.*

*Each day you awake is another day I give you
to do My will. Do not spend your days foolishly,
for My harvest is ripe, and My laborers are few.
(Matthew (9:37-38)*

*You are of greatest service to Me, when you allow Me to use
your life for My glory and not your own.*

*There have been many days when you have run off with the
combine (My word), to bring in the crop yourself.
I appreciate your willingness to bring lost souls into My
Kingdom. You must remember, it is My Spirit that fuels the
truth, not your own strength and wisdom.*

*Allow My Spirit to do the work,
you just need to listen and obey.
Without My Spirit convicting souls and giving you the words,
your efforts will be like a combine without fuel.*

*When you do good works in your own strength,
you receive the glory because they see you and not Me
Let Me work through you, so that others can see Me in you.
Let My people see My mighty works.*

*Never let anyone tell you that you are not of great service to
Me. Your ministry might not be on the platform, but it
doesn't make you or your calling any less important
to Me or My Kingdom.*

*I need all My workers to bring in the crops,
not just My Pastors and Evangelists.*
cc

THE BLIND MAN

Why do you let your troubles control you?
You must come to a point, where you do not see your troubles
for more than what they are.
They are a stepping stone for another victory in your life.

If you are feeling overwhelmed, it is because you have not
given Me proper place in your life. You must let Me help you,
so the winds of life won't blow you over.

The things you think are important, are really not.
You must come to Me continually, so that I can impart to you
My knowledge and strength for your daily life.

It grieves My heart when you turn to a friend for guidance
instead of turning to Me. Do you not yet trust Me?

What is it that you need Me to show you, so that you will
know that part of My joy of being God is to get you ready for
the many things I've called you to do?

I have not given up on you, so why are you so down?
Do you think I won't use you for My kingdom's sake?

My child, it is My desire for you to be a vessel filled with My
power. But first, you must hold still long enough so that I can
empty you of self-works so that you will labor out of
My abilities and not your own...

You must stop second guessing My ability to cleanse you of
the thoughts and actions that hold you in bondage.
(Galatians 5:1) (Romans 8:12-14 and 21)
You have held so much doubt in your heart.

*I would have you be as the blind man; who can't see the
distractions of this world, he trusts in the guidance of his
Seeing Eye dog.*
*Allow My Holy Spirit to be your spiritual Seeing Eye dog. Ask
Him to lead you through the brokenness of this world. Trust
Him to guide you through valleys of doubt and temptations.
Ask Him to reveal to you all truth.*

*How many people are you going to let lead you
before you let My Spirit lead you? Do not rely on others to
give you what I personally want to give to you.*

*Do not let this world lead you away from Me or My Kingdom.
Do not let work, relationships or money come between us.
Do not allow these things to determine your next step.*

*I have called other to help you.
But do not replace your need for Me, with them.*

*Look into My face and be still...
knowing that I have the ability to provide you with all things,
if you would but trust in Me.*

*You have been so blind to the ways of My Kingdom,
and the provisions I have made for you.
(Psalms 139:16)   (2 Peter 1:2-11)
Is it too hard to believe that nothing
is impossible for Me to do?*

*It would be unwise if the blind man left his dog on the curb
and tried to cross the street alone.*

*Just so, My child, it is dangerous crossing into satan's
kingdom without Me. You must rely solely on My Holy Spirit
to guide you, step by step.*

*The moment you "think" it is safe to start walking
by yourself... you will get ran-over.
You must cleave to Me and only Me.*
cc

SACRIFICE YOUR CHOICE

I want to speak to you about fasting.

*Fasting, when done for My sake,
is a tool to prepare you for the discipline needed for the
ministry to which I have called you.*

Let it be a visual reminder of Me and not the temptation.

*Each time you hunger, think of My hunger for My lost
children. Each time your stomach cries out to be fed, think of
My children who are truly starving.
Will you hunger for Me more than what you are fasting?
I want you to see how much you rely
on the food (things) of this world.*

*My child, you have an appetite for so many things
that are not healthy. Many times you have fed on spiritual
things that are not of Me.*

*Are you willing to give up the things you do and desire that
are not of Me? With My strength, you can overcome any
temptation set before you. (I Corinthians 10:13)*

*The sacrifice of your choice not to have or do these things,
shows Me that you are ready to lay your life down so I can
completely reign in you and through you.*

*I desire My children to want Me above anything this world
has to offer. My people have let the ways of this world rule
them, instead of allowing Me the joy of being God.*

*Come before Me and ask what I would have you fast.
Let Me cleanse you of the things
you hold more dear, than Me.
Let your fast be a celebration of your love for Me.*
cc

Stop Back-Biting

My child, you must stop gossiping
and sipping on other people's sorrow.

You must not comment on things you don't understand.

You must not judge My people. That is My job.

Have you forgotten what it felt like when others were using
their tongues against you?

Your tongue has hurt many, do not let your mouth became a
tool for satan's use. (Proverbs 18:20-21)

Each time you judge one of My people by the law of good and
evil, you are sinning against Me. When you act as the judge
and give your opinion towards one of My children, it stops
you from hearing My thoughts toward that person.

You must love My people as I do. (1 Peter 3:10)
Look past the areas in their lives where I have not been
allowed to enter. Pray for them, as others have for you.

Your tongue has wounded many... REPENT NOW!!!

When your tongue complains, about your life or a situation
you are in or the needs you have, you're biting My back!

Stop putting Me down in front of others.
Come to Me and tell Me of the complaints you have.
cc

Ephesians 4:29

"Let no corrupt communication proceed out of your mouth, but that which is good to the use of edifying, that it may minister grace unto the hearers."

I CREATED YOU FOR MY GLORY

*Your jealousy is against Me and not the person you are
jealous of. Each time you hold jealousy in your heart,
you are placing distrust towards Me in your heart.*

*When you are jealous of one of My children,
and what I have given him; you are telling Me you are not
pleased with the life I have given you, or with the many gifts
I hand picked just for you.*

Do you not realize how this grieves My heart?

*I wonder if I should give you more,
if you don't like what I have given you already?
What is it about your life that you do not like?*

*My child, when are you going to realize
that when I made you, I took great thought about what you
were to look like, what talents and spiritual gifts
I wanted you to have?*

*You act as if I closed My eyes when I created you.
(Psalms 139:1-18)*

*I have allowed many trials and sufferings to come into your
life to cause you to realize your need for Me.
To learn to rely on My strength and wisdom
to carry on, not your own. But through it all,
I want your heart to be made beautiful.
(Psalms 71:19-21) (James 1:12) (Hebrews 5:8)*

*Each time you went through heartache and pain,
I was there collecting each tear. (Psalms 56:8)
My child, I love you....
It's time, to deal with what you believe about your life.
Come to Me, and let Me lead you step by step,
out of the valley of self doubt and destruction.*

Your life, My child, has not been a waste.
I will use your experiences to help heal those who are hurting
from the same kind of trials you have already gone through.
(2 Corinthians 1:3-4)

Have I been unfair to you when I created you?
Each cell of your body was created by Me.

Stop believing that the way your physical body works and
looks stops Me from using you for My purpose.

Stop being mad because I didn't create you, the way you
t-h-i-n-k I should have. Give your anger to Me.
Let Me give you the truth, in exchange for your misbelief.

The anger and jealousy you harvest in your heart is an open
door for satan's use. He will use it to step into your life and
cause envy, strife and discontentment.

Ask and I will cleanse your heart of false beliefs
and close the door to jealousy.
I have a reason for the way I beautifully created you.

When you don't feel beautiful on the outside, know that it is
not your outside which is to be beautiful, but the inside of you
which shines with My beauty and glory. It's your heart being
right with Me that makes you beautiful.

Do not think I created you any other way,
than the way I wanted you. Come to a place with Me,
where you can let go of what you wanted to look like and the
things you wanted to have.

Start believing that I don't make mistakes nor junk.

When you see another who is prettier or more handsome,
smaller or bigger, more talented, intelligent or wealthy;
you must stop believing I cheated you in these areas.
Don't hide your feelings of disappointment from Me.
Take them directly to Me so I can speak the truth to you.

*My Son, Jesus, did not find His wealth in money,
nor did He find His worth from man.
He found His worth and wealth in Me.*

I have equipped you to do My will. (John 14:11-13)

*You will get to a point, when you will be able to share in My
joy of how I created another,
instead of comparing yourself with them.*

I have not forgotten one thing when I created you.

*Learn to enjoy yourself and the gifts I have given you.
Do not feel guilty for the things I choose to give you.
Only when you can stop being jealous of what I give to others
can you receive and accept the many things
I want to give to you.*

*When you begin to trust Me enough to know that I didn't
cheat you, you'll rejoice for all of My creation.
There will not be one jealous thought left in your mind.*

*No longer will you put value on the way a person looks, the
ministry they have or the material things they possess.*

Choose joy My child. Truly today is a new day.

*My love for you will strengthen you,
and take you through this period of doubt and distrust.*

*Know that I have a reason and purpose for each person.
I love each one of My children.*

*The less you compare yourself to others, the more you will
begin to trust Me and My choices for you.*

*Stop and enjoy what I have blessed you with,
so that I can give you more. (1 Timothy 4:12-14)*
cc

WORRY

Worry is as a snakebite to your body.
Its venom can paralyze you with fear.

Worry's purpose is to stop you from receiving life from Me.
Worry replaces My truth with lies of disbelief and doubt.

Worry creeps in, to control your thoughts and slowly wraps
around your mind, to squeeze out
the very breath of My Word.

Learn to recognize the sound of the faintest rustling of the
grass, (which is your thoughts becoming troubled) stop what
you are doing and listen for My direction. I will lead you
safely away from the confusion confronting you.

When your mind is full of worry and fear it is because you do
not trust Me with the outcome of your life.

You must not listen to your own thoughts about a situation.
They can deceive you and lead you into a wrong direction,
a road on which I may have not wanted you to walk on.

Be prepared, in case you are struck,
and carry with you the antidote, which is My word.
Come to Me for the truth. I will set you free to run and play
without the fear of being bitten.

You must listen at all times for My direction
because I have the only map for traveling life's road.
You are safest when your holding on to My hand.
I can see the whole picture of Life, not just the hill that's in
front of you this very moment.

Just by My spoken thoughts,
the sun rises each day to awake the world, and sets with
whatever glorious colors I choose.

*Do you not understand that I alone have been given the
authority to rule My people? I know what you need before
you even ask. Why do you still choose to worry over things
that only I can control?*

*Only when you start to trust My decisions and timing,
can you be safe from worry. This My child, is just a small
portion of My strengths and abilities.*

*Do you not realize I Am the Creator of all?
Oh My child, of little faith.
Can you not see? I have much more in store for you, than you
are allowing Me to share with you.*

*You have but tasted My desires for you.
Come and feast of Me and you'll never be the same again.*

*I will fill you with such power and strength.
The kind this world has never seen.
If you will but empty yourself for My use.*

*Just trust, listen, obey and give Me the credit.
If you do these things, My child, there will be nothing of Me
and My Glory that will be hidden from you.
I will give you all that I Am
so that you can bring to Me, My lost sheep.*

*My child, I have chosen you
to do many great things for My Kingdom.
Please accept this knowledge with honor not pride.*

*This does not make you greater than another.
It just means I have given you more responsibility.
(Galatians 5:25-26)*

*You must never boast that the power I give you
is because of anything you did to deserve it.
It is out of the love I have for My people.*

cc

THE BATTLE GROUND

*For some reason you skip past some of the duties I have given
you. You must not think that even My smallest command is
not of the utmost importance to Me.
Following each instruction is crucial for your growth,
obedience and victory over satan.*

*My child, please don't disobey Me, because the moment you
do, satan has won rights to you in that area. He will try to
get that area of disobedience to grow out of control.*

*You must keep all entrances closed to satan.
Do not even look at the temptations he sets before you.
They are just bait to get your eyes off Me.*

*Fill your mind with My words, so that I'm your first thought
of the day. The last thought you think upon at night. My
Words are promises I give to you. You must learn what your
rights are as a child of My Kingdom.
Know the truth of who you are in Me and
satan will no longer be able to slip you lies.*

*Do not go on any longer being burnt out.
Smoke is a signal of fire; depression is a signal of an attack.
Fire produces heat, just as his attack will produce turmoil in
your life. Just as water can put out a fire,
My truth applied will bring you peace and rest.
You must pick up and use the water to put out the fire,
likewise, you must pick up My Bible and believe what it says,
to quench his fiery attacks. (Ephesians 6:10-18)*

*Stand your ground; don't let satan take away the rights My
Son, Jesus, won for you.
Jesus won the battle over sin, death and sickness.
All you need to do is believe and receive My strength
to walk in this victory.*
cc

DEPEND ON ME, NOT YOURSELF

Do not become like Eve and consider the lies of the tempter.
Do not mix a lie with truth, so that the sin sounds better.
I tell you, if Eve would have run to Me instead of the tree,
I would have given her the strength to resist the lie.

Do you not yet realize that the tree of good and evil of which
she ate represents man's pride of believing he can walk with
out Me? Man's belief that I will withhold something "good"
from him.

Each time My people eat from the tree of pride, it shows the
world they don't need Me to govern their lives, that within
themselves they can be god.

Do not be tempted to let pride tell you, you are better or more
together than any of My children. I have not given you the
right to judge. When you judge yourself and others from the
tree of good and evil, you are wearing My shoes.
(Matthew 7:1-5)

I Am the only God this world needs.
I Am the only One who knows the heart of man.
I would ask you today to start eating from My tree of life;
the truth of your need for Me.

You must come to a place in your heart where you realize
your complete need for Me. Do not try to walk in this world
alone. Stop being full of your own beliefs, instead be humble
and depend on My Holy Spirit to continually fill you with My
strength and wisdom. Listen to My truth for your life. You
won't be disappointed. Stop listening to what this "world" is
trying to tell you about your life.

Give all of yourself to Me. The moment you doubt anything,
run to Me, not the world of good and evil for truth.
cc

CONTINUAL FLOW

*If you would but listen to and obey My voice,
you would not even need to stumble.
I do not know why you make life so hard. Listening to My
counsel (advice) instead of others would keep you from going
through unnecessary trials.*

*It is My plan for you to prosper and grow
in My strength and teaching, not your own.
Why must I wait in line for your attention?
Stop trying to hide behind the things of this world.*

*You act as if I were a water faucet. You think that you can
turn Me off and on, and that's how I Am supposed to work.
Let My Spirit flow continually within you.
There is much work that needs to be done
with My Spirit running, not yours.*

*Let Me use your hands to hold - heal My hurting children.
Let Me use your feet to walk to those who can't walk.
Let Me use your ears so you can follow My command.
Let Me use your voice to proclaim My goodness.
Let Me use your time so that I can fill it with My plans.*

*Give to Me, your desires and expectations of the life you want
or expect to have. Let Me replace them with My desires so
that you can truly live in peace trusting Me.*

*Please know that I love you deeply. I eagerly wait daily,
for you to turn to Me and not others.*

*Please don't limit Me, tune Me out or shut Me off.
Let Me have complete access into your life.
What a glorious day it will be when you trade in your
thoughts for Mine. Allowing Me to be glorified throughout
each day I give you.*

cc

I AM WAITING

*I have waited so long for My people
to allow Me the role they have been playing.
To let Me really guide their direction.*

*I long for My people to come to Me daily. Seeking My
direction and desire for their lives each day.*

*So many times you have run off to start your day without
even a spoken word to Me. Please don't speak to Me out of
ritual, speak to Me out of your heart.*

*I created you to need Me more
than you need the air to breathe.*

*I must have the very breath of your being
in union with Mine.*

*My love is greater than words can express.
Words alone are not sufficient to tell of My love,
but the sacrifice of My Son's shed blood is.
(1 Peter 1:2-5)*

*Please try and understand that I do not need you to carry
guilt for the things you t-h-i-n-k you need to do.*

*I need you to allow Me to work in you and through you so
that I can have the joy of sharing the task with you.*

*When you thank Me for the work I have done through you,
I receive the Glory, not you.
The only Glory I want you to receive is from Me.
Let Me be the one to edify you, not the world.*

*Please offer up your fleshly desires and ideas so that they can
become a pleasing sacrifice that sets you free.
(1 Peter 2:5)*

My precious child, I have so much in store for you.
Open up your soul to Me and allow Me to pour out My Spirit,
so you can receive all I have for you.

Don't limit what I can do through a willing vessel. Don't turn
away those who don't seem to be likely candidates.

It is not the size, age or color that determines who I will use;
it is their yieldedness to My Spirit.

Allow Me the privilege of directing your life for My Glory.

When I speak, will you listen?
When I ask, will you obey?

When I move, will you go with Me,
or will you stay in your comfort zone?
Are you willing to risk all for Me?
cc

Acts 2:17-18

"'And in the last days it shall be, God declares, that I will pour out My Spirit on all flesh, and your sons and your daughters shall prophesy, and your young men shall see visions, and your old men shall dream dreams; even on My male servants and female servants in those days I will pour out My Spirit, and they shall prophesy.

Romans 8:13-14

For if you live according to the flesh you will die, but if by the Spirit you put to death the deeds of the body, you will live. For all who are led by the Spirit of God are sons of God.

Volume III

LET ME BE THE TEACHER

There is a learning time for everything in My Kingdom.
I will teach you all that I would have you to know
about Me and My kingdom.

Your eagerness to grow pleases Me.
But you must remember,
I Am the teacher, and you are the student.

I want you to follow My lessons, and not your own.
I have laid out each one carefully
and with much thought.

Make sure as you study My Word, you allow My Holy Spirit,
to study with you. He is your Tutor.
(1 John 2:27)

A lesson will only be too hard
if you try to do it by yourself.

Do not skip past a lesson,
believing that you already have the answers.
Learn to lean on My wisdom, not your own.

Please don't be afraid of failing.
I will only test and correct you after I know you have an
understanding of what I've taught you.

I do not look at failure, I look at growth. Your weaknesses
are opportunities for growth. Allow Me to correct the areas
of your life you need growth in.
Your strengths, unless given to Me, will stop your growth.

I have allowed time for you to grow,
so be patient with your growth.

Remember, you are so special to Me.
Your zeal to please Me is exciting, but don't get discouraged
and stop trying a lesson
if you don't do it perfectly the first time.

Perfection to Me is, when one relies on Me completely.

So, if you're doing something perfectly for Me,
it's not the product I want to see perfect.
It's your mind being completely free to focus on what I have
asked you to do.

A human heart can only reach perfection when it completely
trusts Me enough to do everything I ask.

You must tune into My voice, so that it's all you'll hear
throughout the day. No longer will you hear your own
thoughts. You will take charge over them.
No seed of fear, doubt, selfishness or rebellion will be left in
your heart or mind.

No longer will satan effectively tempt you; he will flee in fear
from you. He will have tested you in every area of your life,
and he will find nothing left in you that is his.
I will have a completely clean vessel for My use.

Oh, My child, let My Holy Spirit be your life long Tutor.
For it will take all of eternity for My children to learn
everything about Me and My Kingdom.

Each day is a new beginning in My forever Kingdom.

Enjoy each day, because there is a lesson I want you to learn
or master. It might be hidden behind all the tasks of the day,
but take time to look for what I want to teach you that day. It
might be a lesson on patience or it could be one on jealousy or
even one on resting in My Presence.
Whatever the lesson, rely on My Holy Spirit
to guide you through it.

Do not let the dogs of this world chew up your homework.
Seal it with the protection of My Holy Spirit, so nothing can
take away what you have learned.

Don't be afraid to stop and raise your hand for help.
I Am never to busy to answer your questions.
I will never make fun of you,
no matter how silly the question might seem to you.
All I ask is that you listen for the answer.

Oh, My child, learn your lessons quickly. Don't drop out;
I have so many plans for you after graduation.

Your graduation from "college" comes when you are able to
yield to My every thought and desire;
obeying Me throughout the entire day.

Then, I will unleash My awesome
miracle-working power in you,
and you will use it for My Glory and not your own.
cc

Proverbs 3:5-6

Trust in the LORD with all your heart, and do not lean on your own understanding. In all your ways acknowledge Him, and He will make straight your paths.

Romans 8:14-22

"For I consider that the sufferings of this present time are not worth comparing with the glory that is to be revealed to us. For the creation waits with eager longing for the revealing of the sons of God. For the creation was subjected to futility, not willingly, but because of him who subjected it, in hope that the creation itself will be set free from its bondage to corruption and obtain the freedom of the glory of the children of God."

MISTAKES

*If a three year old child colored you a picture,
and presented it to you as a gift, what would you tell her?*

*Do you point out that she colored out of the lines, or do you
thank her for the gift she has made for you?*

*You would look past the scribble marks,
and tell her she did a wonderful job.
This would not be a lie, because you saw her love and
commitment, behind the picture as it was being made.*

*To correct her and tell her she did not do a good job
at this point would crush her. (She truly did her best).
You realize, with more practice, she will be able to color
within all the lines beautifully.*

I Am no different.

*When you truly do your best and fall short
I don't look at the mistakes.
I look at your heart, which is more beautiful, than the act you
wanted to do for Me.*

*When you give your best to Me, out of love and not
selfishness; I Am truly pleased, no matter how many mistakes
you think you have made.*

A mistake to Me is proof you tried.

*I will teach you all that I would have you to know.
I will have you practice doing the very thing I want you to
learn, so do not skip past the practice that is needed
to become like My Son.*

Please don't be afraid of making a mistake.

I will only hold you accountable and correct you,
after you know how to do what I have asked.

I have allowed time for you to grow.
Do not become discouraged when you have tried your best
and still color out of the lines.

I know that you have a pest trying
to get you to step out of My guidelines for your life.

Remember, I see the whole picture,
not just the scribble marks.

Come to Me and ask for My help.

Yes, soon you will be able to walk
within all My ways, as My Son did.

First We need to eliminate your play time
With the "pest" (Satan).

Give up all your worldly ideas and wants;
shut every door to satan.

Let Me fill you with My desires.
Let My Kingdom fulfill your needs.
cc

Romans 8:29-30

For those whom He foreknew He also predestined to be
conformed to the image of His Son, in order that He might be
the firstborn among many brothers. And those whom He
predestined He also called, and those whom He called He also
justified, and those whom He justified He also glorified.

Do Not Let Your Mind Be Overloaded

Oh, My precious child, I have so much in store for you.
Allow Me the privilege of sharing My dreams with you.
(Psalms 139:13-16)

If I Am bringing you to a place that is unfamiliar;
don't be afraid. When it's the darkest,
My light of glory will shine the brightest.
Please don't try to figure out all the details.
Leave that to Me.

I love surprising you with My goodness.

If you feel a little uncertain about the direction
I Am taking your life, this is good.
Preconceived ideas about your future will make it much
harder for you to accept My perfect will for your life.

Learn to trust Me with all.

Do not withhold any thoughts, doubts,
anger or sin from Me.

When you start to hide yourself from Me,
you will start to feel alone and troubled. Everything you feel
and go through in the day is important to Me.
Do not let the actions of the day come between us.

Do not fret over what you are to do
for Me and My kingdom.

I will provide all that is necessary
to complete the work that I give you.
Remember, it is I completing the work through you.
Please don't make it a burden by trying to do everything by
yourself. Hand the work load back to Me,

let My Spirit feed you with strength.
You must allow yourself to receive
of My goodness and mercy.

Do not withhold from your spirit,
the daily infilling of My Spirit.

I Am your God...
Allow My love to protect you from the dangers of worry.

Cast all your burdens and cares created by this world, to Me.
Allow My Spirit to gently caress away
the tension felt in your mind.
(1 Peter 5:6-7)

You need not fear the future I have chosen for you.

My child, I Am forever with you,
and My angels are camped around you
night and day to ensure your safety.
(Psalms 34:7)
cc

Psalms 91:9-16

Because you have made the LORD your dwelling place The Most High, who is my refuge-- no evil shall be allowed to befall you, no plague come near your tent. For He will command His angels concerning you to guard you in all your ways. On their hands they will bear you up, lest you strike your foot against a stone. You will tread on the lion and the adder; the young lion and the serpent you will trample underfoot. "Because He holds fast to Me in love, I will deliver him; I will protect him, because he knows My name. When he calls to Me, I will answer him; I will be with him in trouble; I will rescue him and honor him. With long life I will satisfy him and show him My salvation."

Relax

You must not compare your past with your present.

*Each day I bring you is unique. Do not allow old thoughts
and feelings to tell you what each day will bring.*

*Let me surprise you with My goodness.
Give to Me each day, the troubles you face.*

*You have become so tired.
You have expected so much of yourself.*

*You have allowed your beliefs
to tell you what you should or shouldn't be doing.
Listen to Me, not yourself.*

*Have I caused you this anguish? No. It's your thoughts and
feelings holding you into bondage.*

*Recognize what your thoughts and expectations are.
Your own expectations will overwhelm you.
Mine will lift you up and encourage you.*

*I bring strength to you, not weakness.
It is through My strength that you see your weakness.
But do not embrace the weakness; embrace Me.
(2 Corinthians 12:19)*

*While I Am holding you, you act as if you are drowning.
In your own effort to save yourself,
you become weaker and more fearful.*

*Rest and relax in My arms.
Enjoy the life I have given you.
Stop struggling and realize how much I love you!*
cc

SATAN HAS NO POWER

I surround you with My love and protection.

Would you let your child fall,
if he asked you to hold his hand?

With Me there are no accidents.
Trust in Me and you will have the protection you need.

I long for you to truly enjoy life.
I do not want you to live in fear and doubt.

I will give you the desires of your heart, when you realize that
I Am the One that put those desires there.

Trust Me and believe that I will
use your complete life for My Glory.
(Psalms 37:4-5)

Be not troubled when you feel
that I Am not using you on the front line.

Do not feel as if I left you out or that you're not good enough
for My use.

I will, with each of My children's help,
win back My lost people.

No longer will My heart be filled with pain and grief.

My Son died and rose
to stop the power satan had over My people.

Do not be afraid of satan when you're holding My hand.

Do not let him intimidate with fear;
satan was stripped of all his power.

My Son has given you the authority... (Luke 10:18-20)

Pray with one another, and for one another.

My Son is the Savior, and you are His chosen generation.

*Do you not realize there is nothing you could do
to make Me love you more, than I already do?*

*Stop trying to please Me through works.
Your love for Me alone pleases Me.*
cc

Mark 6:13

And they cast out many demons and anointed with oil many who were sick and healed them.

Mark 16:15-30

Go ye into all the world, and preach the gospel to the whole creation. Whoever believes and is baptized will be saved, but whoever does not believe will be condemned. And these signs will accompany those who believe: in My name they will cast out demons; they will speak in new tongues; they will pick up serpents with their hands; and if they drink any deadly poison, it will not hurt them; they will lay their hands on the sick, and they will recover." So then the Lord Jesus, after he had spoken to them, was taken up into heaven and sat down at the right hand of God. And they went out and preached everywhere, while the Lord worked with them and confirmed the message by accompanying signs.

Luke 10:18-20

Behold, I have given you authority to tread on serpents and scorpions, and over all the power of the enemy, and nothing shall hurt you. Nevertheless, do not rejoice in this, that the spirits are subject to you, but rejoice that your names are written in heaven."

The Storms of Life

My sweetest possession in all creation is you.
(Deuteronomy 14:2)

You bring Me such pleasure and joy.
Let Me be a joy to you.

Let your thoughts not stray, even for a moment, away from My guidance and love. Let My love dwell within you.

You can not truly love another,
until My love is the One loving them.

Oh, how My people have labored out of self.
Let your work be done out of My Unconditional Love.

You need so desperately, to be filled with My love.

My Love is the cure to the pain
that satan's dominion has caused.

Please hold still, while I conform you into My likeness.
Trust Me when I Am fine tuning you.
I Am forming you into a pure vessel, with a heart large enough to store the love that My Spirit will pour into you.

Let not one part of your being be filled with self.

I want everything you do,
to come from My strength, not your own.

Be still and rest in Me through each storm.
(Romans 8:28) (1 Peter 4:19)

You are My child, and I Am the Mighty King who rules over all things. Let Me reveal to you what this means.

Each time that you take your destiny into your own hands,
you find yourself in a whirlwind of confusion.
I will help you to stand through the storms of life.
You must realize that it is I who control the winds.
(Matthew 8:23-27) (Psalms 89:9)

Allow Me the captain's chair.
Let Me steer your vessel,
I Am the only One Who truly knows
where you are supposed to go.

The waves of fear and doubt had almost drowned you.
The rocks of sin had almost crushed you.
The winds of anger had almost destroyed you.
The net of jealousy had you trapped.

This was not My plan for you;
but through all of these trials you ran to man and not Me.

I forgive you, My precious child,
for your lack of trust in Me.

All along I was as the lighthouse, standing strong, not moved
by any storm; gently you began to let My light reach your
darkness and you began to see
a tower of strength in Me.

I Am glad you have realized that the only way to make it
through the storms is to rely on My direction and
let Me steer you along the way.

I Am pleased that you have allowed Me
to save your drowning ship.
I will restore your vessel greater than before;
because you have now realized that you can't be the captain
of your ship, only I can.

As your captain I will not steer your vessel into more than
you can handle. I know where you are to sail.

*Let Me launch you. Do not try to push yourself into the ocean
when I have not yet finished your ship.
No, I would not let you sink, but you would not have all of the
equipment on board that you need for your journey.*

Right now, allow Me the time to prepare you.

*When you are ready,
there will be nothing in this world that can stop or change the
course on which I will steer you.*

*Have joy, your ship is about ready to sail.
But this time, allow Me to be the captain.
Let Me give the orders. I will never steer you wrong.
Trust Me so completely that when you are in a storm,
know that I have allowed it to test your sails.
I do not want any area of your sail to go unchecked by Me.*

*You must not try to hide even the smallest sin from Me.
If you do not yield all of your weaknesses to Me and let Me
replace them with My strength, satan will shred the very part
of your sail (life) that you did not hand to Me.*

*When I send you out to reach My lost, no storm
(attempt from satan) will be able to stop you,
if you let Me be in charge of your life.*

*Trust in Me, My child,
All is well.*
cc

Ephesians 4:14-15

So that we may no longer be children, tossed to and fro by the waves and carried about by every wind of doctrine, by human cunning, by craftiness in deceitful schemes. Rather, speaking the truth in love, we are to grow up in every way into Him who is the head, into Christ.

Come Soar With Me

*A heart totally yielded to My Holy Spirit is like a kite, yielded
to the wind. A kite by itself will never fly.
Just as you, My child, will never soar as an eagle
without My Spirit.*

*A kite's security is in the string
that holds it from being blown away.
What have you allowed to be your security?
In what have you put your faith and trust?*

*Let My Son be your string, security and life-line.
Trust Me with where My Winds will take you.*

*But I caution you,
do not let circumstances hold the string to your life.
Do not let your time schedule tell you whether or not you have
time to come away and fly with Me.*

*My child, there is no reason why you should
ever have to leave My Presence.*

*Do not let the duties of the day
become as bricks lying on your kite.
Release all your worries and responsibilities to Me
so you can soar again. (Hebrews 12:1-2)*

*I will not let the power lines entangle you,
nor let thunder storms strike you down.
Have you forgotten, I also control the winds?*

*Come to Me without fear. Let Me untangle the thoughts that
hold you in bondage, so that you may fly higher.*

*Picture each sin, burden or distraction as a string.
How many strings do you have tugging on you?*

Hand each one over to My Son,
and He will cut them loose from your life.

As you become One with My Son,
you will know how to rest in Me.

Your kite will be able to soar through anything.
If you will rest upon My Word, trusting US to guide you
through, knowing I Am in control as long as you let Me be.

Once you learn how to rest in Me,
you will get to know the rest of Me.

I LOVE YOU...
cc

Isaiah 40:31

But they who wait for the LORD shall renew their strength; they shall mount up with wings like eagles; they shall run and not be weary; they shall walk and not faint.

Matthew 11:28-30

Come to Me, all who labor and are heavy laden, and I will give you rest. Take My yoke upon you, and learn from Me, for I am gentle and lowly in heart, and you will find rest for your souls. For My yoke is easy, and My burden is light."

REINS OF YOUR LIFE

My child, you can not live by "what ifs."
You must be certain it is I,
who tells you to step in a certain direction.
Let Me have the reins to your life.

I continually whisper My love to you through out the day.
Take time to listen to the beauty I Am sharing with you.

There is not one duty you have throughout the day
that I don't want to be included in.
In each activity, I have something I wish to reveal to you.
Let Me feed you throughout the day.

I know how the tasks of the day,
tug at your heart and mind for attention.

When you start to feel overwhelmed, give your attention to
Me. At that moment, I will speak the words
which will free your mind to be at peace.

Turn your thoughts over to Me
continually throughout the day.

If you'll allow Me to,
I will take each thought and place them where
I think they should go in your life.

Some of the thoughts you keep hold of should be put in the
garbage can. They are of no use to your spiritual growth.

Let Me have the reins to the wild thoughts that possess you.
Let nothing possess your mind unless it is the pondering of
My words throughout the day.

When a burden is disturbing you,
give it immediately to Me.

Don't be tempted to think that I can't help you
or that I'm too busy or not interested in your "laundry".
I Am interested in anything that
takes your thoughts and mind from Me.

When I say "bring all your burdens to Me" I mean ALL,
not just the one you think you can't handle.
I want the ones you think you can handle, because those are
the ones that are disturbing you the most.

How do you expect Me to instruct you when you won't let Me
on the saddle? Each time you let Me into your corral, you
won't hold still long enough for Me to put the reins on.

Why do you fear My leading?
Do I have to ride your pride to the point you break?
When can I trust you not to buck Me off?

When can I take the reins off,
knowing you will follow the leading of My commands?

I have bred you to be strong,
but not strong enough to live without Me.

I will not force you to do anything,
but you must be well trained and mannered
before I enter you into the arena of a warrior's life.
cc

Psalms 32:8-9

I will instruct you and teach you in the way you should go; I will counsel you with My eye upon you. Be not like a horse or a mule, without understanding, which must be curbed with bit and bridle, or it will not stay near you.

WHOSE SEED DO YOU HAVE PLANTED?

Each time you disobey Me, a seed of rebellion is planted.
For each sin there is a seed that gets planted
in the soil of your heart.

If you do not repent;
the seed will grow as fast as it is being watered,
however, the moment you ask Me to forgive you,
I will chop down your tree of sin no matter how big it is.

Any seed you have planted, whether it is a seed of jealousy,
doubt, pride, hate, witchcraft or distrust in Me - no matter
what it is, I will dig it out and till your soil.
(Jeremiah 33:8)

My words are also seeds.
If you allow them to grow in your heart,
they will produce the fruit of My Spirit. (Galatians 5:22)

When turmoil has hit your life, whose fruit hits the ground?
Does anger come out or does peace hold you together?
Does doubt fall to the ground or does faith?

Understand that whatever you hold deep within your heart,
will come to the surface when your life is shaken.

Unholy thoughts, desires or feelings not dealt with,
will mature into sin. (James 1:14-15)

I want you to see whether or not you have any evil roots
still left in your soul. The only way to do this is to test your
fruit when life has shaken you up.

I can see what's left in your heart, but do you?

Come to Me, this day. Let Me gently shake your life,
so that you will see what fruit you are producing.

*Keep in mind, Satan also knows how to inspect
the circumstances of your life, seeing if there is any area
in which he can nurture and plant more seeds of destruction.*

*You must have complete trust in Me
If you don't, the moment you think
(keep in mind the word think, for this is a mind battle)
I have deserted you; Satan will be the one watering your
thoughts, not I.*

*Feed your soul My thoughts. My word lives.
It brings life to all those who read it and believe it.
Let it give you strength, when you are under attack.*

*My fruit will grow in you, as it is My desire,
but you must first plant My seed, which is My word.
Do not sow your crop sparingly.
My Bible is a seed tree; I want you to shake each page,
so that you can receive each seed of, Who I Am.*

*As you allow My Holy Spirit to plant seeds of truth
in your heart and soul, you will become free
to see who you are in Me.*

*But know that when the seed is first planted, if it's not planted
deep, the wind (satan) can blow and take it away. You must
water the promises and freedom you receive, with praises to
Me. Your acknowledgment will help pack the truth down into
your soul. (Matthew 13:3-9)*

*The land of the past, you have not allowed Me to sift through,
is held tight with weeds and stones.
(Lies that you believe and areas of doubt and distrust)
My words are stolen in these areas.*

*I caution you My child,
to prepare the soil of your heart before you plant.
There may be a lot of weeds of doubt, roots of bitterness and
stones from the past, left in your heart.*

*Some of you have planted many times, but you did not receive
the crop that was due, because the ground of your heart,
was not made fertile.*

*Let Me help you plow out the past hurts and pains.
Together, We will replant your soil.
Your heart will be filled with all My fruits, not just a few.
(John 15:4-16)*

*Allow Me, to till the soil of your past.
Let Me remove the sorrow and pain that lie there.*

*I came into this world to set you free
from the bondage that has entangled you.*

*Trust Me, for I Am the expert gardener, I Am the one who
created and cultivated the Earth with all its splendor.
Do you not think I know how to build My temple in you?*

*What man has destroyed in selfishness,
I will rebuild with love.*

*A day is coming when I will plow the Earth to rid it of all the
weeds of wickedness. It will be again a place of My perfect
harmony, because I will be ruler, not man.
(Matthew 13:24-30)*

*Please come to Me today and let My love for you,
break through the pavement of anger and resentment that
has hardened in your heart and mind.*

*Your faith in Me, waters the seeds for your harvest.
My perfect love casts out all seeds of fear.
(1 John 4:18)*

*I LOVE YOU!!!
cc*

SURRENDER

I would have you reach into the depths of your heart
and hand Me the things you hold more dear, than Me.

Do not fool yourself in believing you have given all to Me.
There are places in your heart
that you have not let Me rule.

I need every fiber of your being in tune with Mine.

My child, I wait for the day when you will
love Me with your complete mind, soul and strength.
(Deuteronomy 6:5)

In the meantime, many of My people are missing a part of
Me, which needs to be seen in you.

Release all to Me.
Do not hide one thought or feeling from Me.

Come to Me with all honesty; tell Me how you really feel.

Do not hide behind idle words.
Let your mouth express the cries of your heart.

Do not let your mind interfere
with what your heart has to say.

Open up to Me, so I can set you free
from the thoughts that hold you down.

Let Me remove the stones of doubt and distrust that are
blocking you from loving Me completely.

I love you so much and I await your complete surrender.
cc

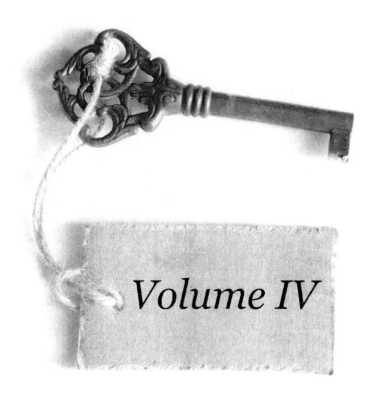

Volume IV

Rest In Me

Please stop running away from Me each time you pray and
My presence brings you a sense of freedom and direction.
Just because you listened one day to Me,
doesn't mean you don't have to listen, the next.

I have not created you to walk alone.

Each time I give you a desire,
you run with it but away from Me. Why is this so?
Are you afraid that I will not
fulfill the desires I have placed in your heart?
Do you believe I Am teasing you with My goodness?

You must stop your mind from running from Me.
My child, I want to share with you all things.

When you listen only when you want to,
My heart is torn.

My child, you are so close but yet so far.
It is My desire for you to walk in My presence,
continually throughout each day.

Learn to trust My voice.
Will you allow Me to fill your mind,
with My thoughts instead of your own?
You rely so much on your own strength and wisdom.

My child, take rests and learn to rely on My strengths. So
many times you struggle and squirm trying to please Me.
Do you not yet realize that nothing is more pleasing
then when you rest and wait on Me?

I long to give you strength and direction for your next task.
Let Me fill you to overflowing.
Let My love and peace surround you so that no matter how
big the task is, you remain calm.

Do not rely on yourself. I did not give you enough strength to
walk without Me. I made you to need Me.
Do not be ashamed of your weakness.
Admit your need for Me.

When you ignore Me throughout the day, you become tired
and upset with the world and all the work you feel you need
to do. I never wanted you to think that the work I have given
you to do, could be done without Me.

My child, how tired you have become. Rest, while I hold you.
Do not struggle to get out of My arms.

You are worthy of love in My eyes.
You do not need to prove your worth to Me or to the world.

Do not be afraid to be still before Me. (Psalms 16:11)

I do not require you to work all the time.
Learn to relax in My presence,
during the storms and the quiet times.
Trust that I have everything under control.

Do not run off to do more work,
before you are filled with My Holy Spirit.
(Exodus 31:3) (Micah 3:8)
(Acts 2:4 - 4:31 - 9:14 - 13:9 - 13:13-52)
(Ephesians 5:17)

I'm your boss, and I Am telling you to take breaks to rest.
I own all the time in the world. Be not afraid, that if you rest,
the work will not be completed on time.

I hold the calendar of eternity.
Learn to trust My perfect timing.
(2 Samuel 22:31) (Isaiah 25:1)
cc

TRUST MY TIMING

I have so much of Myself to share with you.
Allow Me the privilege of sharing My deepest thoughts
and desires for you and My people.

Permit My Spirit to consume your soul.
Oh My child, don't be afraid.

Don't bring up past experiences and failures.
They are not your present.
Fear is not what I have in store for you.

Trust Me with your life.
Let Me lead your every step,
as the Father does with his daughter on her wedding day.

Let Me prepare you Bride, for My Son's coming.
Let Me teach you what is pleasing to Him.
(Revelation 19:7-9)

I Am the One who will wash your garment
and iron out the wrinkles. (Ephesians 5:27)

Please trust that My leading is at the right pace.
I will not rush you too quickly, or walk you too slowly.
My timing is perfect; all you need to do is hold My hand.

Let My Power and Glory flow from your finger tips.
Let Me walk with your legs to My people who won't let Me
near them. Let Me use your hands to touch those who haven't
felt My presence. Let Me use your mouth to speak of My love.
Let Me use your eyes to show you the souls
of My lost children.

Please don't walk without Me. (Psalms 23)
cc

Ministry

*You must at all times be ready to minister
My Son's love to My people.*

*So many of My people believe that to minister
you must have a badge on and a place of "ministry."
(2 Corinthians 3:5-6)*

I say, listen to Me and not others.

*My child, wherever your feet go, so do Mine.
I Am where you are.*

Allow Me to touch My people through your hands.

*Any place you go can be a place I choose for you to minister.
Learn to trust Me more in this area.*

*I will give you the words.
I will show you how to minister to My people.*

*There are so many of My hurting children
whom the church world has ignored.*

*Do not try to pick out for yourself the ones I want you to
minster My love to. Only I know when the hearts of My
people are truly hungry.*

*Allow Me to show you the souls that are ready
to receive freedom from this world's bondage.*

*Some of My people will choose to eat all that you give them.
Others will choose to eat very little, or not all.*

*Do not allow your flesh to become offended,
for it is My feast they refuse to eat.*

Do not be afraid to feed them My Spirit,
no matter how lowly and ungroomed they appear to be.

Do you not yet understand that the pounding in your chest
is My heart leaping for joy over being able to touch
one of My children?

Learn to recognize that the tugging of your heart
is Me pulling you towards that person.

Do not turn away in disbelief.
Do not reason with your flesh.
Do not listen to the fears and allow them to be your master.
Do not walk away from those who need Me the most.
Do not rely on your abilities. Rely on Mine.

My child, can you not see the importance of My people?
My Kingdom should not be limited to just the churches.
Do you not believe the scripture that says?
My Kingdom will be on Earth too?

When I gave you the authority to walk over snakes,
scorpions and all the power of the enemy,
what did you think that meant?

Do not be ignorant and believe that you have to get
permission to do what I have asked you to do.

Whose authority do you need? Man's or Mine?

Do not let your eyes pass over
those who are crying out in their spirit for Me.
Do not be tempted to believe that you alone can fill them.
Do not look at their flesh and think you are better.

I need you to have My complete compassion
for My lost and hurting.
Only when you can love them with My heart,
can you truly love.

Show My people My love
and not your pride and prejudices.
(Romans 12:9-21)

How are My lost going to trust Me if they can't trust you?

Do not fool yourself
into believing that they can't see behind your words.

Let them see Me behind your words.
Let My Spirit have union with theirs.

Do not exalt yourself by believing you are their savior.
Allow My Son to take away their burdens and sin.
(John 7:18)

Give them the truth of My Son, so they can be set free.
Give them the opportunity to accept My Son as Savior.
Give them the hope you have in Me.
Give them the gift that no man or demon can steal.

They may open it in front of you or chose to open it alone.
Even if they never chose to open it at all, you were still
obedient and delivered to them the gift of My Son.
(Romans 6:23)

Won't you please be the hands
I use to minister to My people?
cc

Ephesians 2:8-10

For by grace are ye saved through faith; and that not of yourselves: it is the gift of God: Not of works, lest any man should
boast. For we are his workmanship, created in Christ Jesus
unto good works, which God hath before ordained that we
should walk in them.

Is This Really My Church?

My heart longs to be One with My lost.
But first, I need to be One with My Church.
I need My Church to allow Me, My rightful place.

So many times I have been left out
on the door step of My Churches.
When will you let Me in for longer than a song or two?
Do you believe that a few prayers to Me,
means that I Am in charge?

I need to be allowed the freedom to orchestrate My people for
My use not your own.

Whose Church is it? Whose spirit runs it?
Surely it hasn't completely been Mine.
My Spirit isn't afraid to step out of man-made rituals.
My Spirit brings freedom to all
those who will seek My Face.

I came for the sick, but you cast them away.
(Matthew 9:9-13)
Can you not see that the lost need Me to make them whole?

Would I send away or condemn the "sinner"
because he does not have the ability to clean himself up?
(Luke 7:36-50)

Many of My people believe they have cleaned up their sin.
I would say they are not holy
but bound to pride and to works.

Who has made you righteous? (Romans 10:3-4)
Was it your ability to do good?
Or was it My grace and love? (Titus 3:4-7)

*How can my lost trust Me when they get despised and
rejected from the Church? (Romans 10:11-13)
Are you not to be an example of My love and compassion?
Did I reject you while you were in the depths of sin?*

*Has it been so long that you have forgotten what it felt like to
be in bondage to sin?*

*To those of you who have lead a "good" life
and believe you have no sin; let Me expose it to you.*

*My Church, do you realize what you have done to My people
because of your judgments?*

*How many of My lost are going to have to starve to death
spiritually, before you stop condemning those who don't have
the ability to clean themselves up enough to be
allowed to continue to go to My Church? (John 8:7)*

*Are you afraid that your image as a church
will look bad, if you allow a man still in sin
to come to your "church" on a regular basis?
If that was the case I would have no church,
because there wouldn't be anyone that would "qualify" to go.*

*Whose doctrine are you following? Man's or Mine?
(Matthew 15:8-9)*

*Did I not say to forgive 70 times 7? What did you think that meant?
(Matthew 18:21-35) (Acts 7:59-60)*
cc

James 4:11-12

Do not speak evil against one another, brothers. The one who
speaks against a brother or judges his brother, speaks evil
against the law and judges the law. But if you judge the law,
you are not a doer of the law but a judge. There is only one
lawgiver and judge, He who is able to save and to destroy. But
who are you to judge your neighbor?

I AM YOUR SHEPHERD

Be not dismayed child, I Am still with you.
Do not run from My love.

Why do you believe My love is conditional?
For My judgment is out of righteousness, not hate.

I do not turn My face from you. I turn it from sin.
No matter what sin you are holding on to,
I Am still holding on to you.

It is My wish that you would have no sin in your life.
Come to Me and let Me
remove the dependence you have on sin.

You must be able to turn to Me and
Do not fear intimacy with Me. I will never turn you away.
(Deuteronomy 31:8)

My sheep hear my voice. Are you not one of My Sheep?
(John 10:27-30)

Would a Shepherd reject and push away one of his sheep that
strayed into the wolf's den?
No! He would run to rescue his lost sheep.
Likewise, I will never push you away
when you stray from Me. (Luke 15:4)

I Am watching out for you at all times.
If you would let Me, I would direct your every step.

Many times, I have warned you of danger
and yet you still chose to go your own way.
Did I turn you away or did you turn Me away?
Please, if the wolf (satan) is chasing and harassing you,
run to Me. I will not let him harm you.

It's a cruel, cold world if you try to walk it alone.
Do not let the "wolf" sweet talk you into believing
that in his world of sin, the grass is greener.
Do not let him scare you into believing that your Shepherd
will not take care of your needs or that you have strayed too
far away to be rescued. (Matthew 18:12-13)

Oh, My sheep, when are you going to realize
how much I love you?

Do not walk away from Me any longer.
Do not turn to sin just because the world around you does.
Do not let the momentary pleasures of sin
lure you away from Me.

I have the ability to provide everything you need,
including love. Do not be afraid of My correction
and guidance in your life. I will feed you and give you
strength for your journey.

When you are weary,
ask yourself if you are using your strength or Mine?
(Matthew 11:28-30)

My child, how many times do you have to be bitten and
snipped at before you trust and use
My Wisdom and strength, instead of your own?

Not listening to My voice, even once,
can lead you off of My path of righteousness.
How long will it be and what will it take before you return?

Listen to My voice and I will lead you to still waters
so you can drink in the life I have chosen for you.
The life I have chosen for you is abundantly filled with peace,
love and provision. Not doubt, fear and lack.

Remember, I love you at all times,
not just when you behave. (Isaiah 53:6-7)
cc

Freedom from Guilt and Shame

My child, there have been so many times
you have missed My call.

Please don't labor out of guilt and try to make up for it.

Ask for My forgiveness and be done with it.

You have not understood a valuable lesson.
It's not by your might nor strength but by My Spirit.
(Zechariah 4:6)

Think much on what this means.

I know your flesh is weak.
If you turn to Me, My Spirit of strength will help you
overcome any weakness or temptation.

Do not hide like Eve did when faced with temptation.

Turn to Me so that I can strengthen you.

Do you not realize that I know
what is in your heart and what you're thinking?
(Ezekiel 11:5)

Can you not see it's impossible for you to really hide
your sins from Me? But when you believe you can,
you continue to live in shame because of your thoughts and
feelings. So why do you try to hide?

Be not embarrassed or prideful, bring all to Me.

Please don't try to look good in front of Me
by putting on a mask.

*My eyes of love see right through the ugliness of
sinful thoughts and deeds.*

*I know your deepest secrets and love you anyway.
Won't you confess them to Me, so I can remove the guilt and
shame, hidden in the core of your heart?*

Be honest with yourself and Me.

*What good is it for Me to remove the sin,
if you don't realize you have been set free?*

*It is your own mind that will not let you forget.
(Jeremiah 31:34)*

*I want you to be aware
of all that you have been set free from.
Rejoice at the freedom you have in Me.
(Psalms 51)*

I will take away your guilt and shame. Just ask.
cc

Psalms 32:5

Then I acknowledged my sin to You and did not conceal my
iniquity. I said, "I will confess my transgressions to the LORD,"
and You took away the guilt of my sin. Selah

Share With Me

My dearest one,
I see your pain and frustration.
Why do you choose to carry most of it alone?

I have longed to have intimate conversations with you.
I long to release you from the mental bondages
you have been in.

My child, stop letting guilt come between you and Me.
(Romans 8:1)

I know your heart is to be one with Me.

I Am here with you now, not just in Church.

Lean on Me. Rely on Me to get you through your day.

I Am not keeping a score card
on how many times you go to Church.

My heart just longs to spend time with you
no matter where you are.

You have so many wounds that need to be healed. Will you
trust Me enough to let Me into the core of your heart?

My Child, do not live in shame any longer.

Stop listening to your own opinions.
Listen to Me and what I have to say about your life.

My love, compassion and desire for you are unending.
(Psalms 40:5)

Nothing you could or couldn't do,
can take My love from you.

Stop thinking you are displeasing to Me.
It is not what you do or don't do for Me that pleases Me.
It's the love you have for Me, that brings Me pleasure.

Release all of your frustrations to Me.
Do not walk any longer without Me.

Let Me wipe the tears of loneliness and anger away.
Do not hide how the situations in your
life have caused you pain.

You need to realize the areas of your heart
that are still angry at Me.

Be not ashamed.
I LOVE YOU!
cc

Romans 8:38-39

For I am sure that neither death nor life, nor angels nor rulers, nor things present nor things to come, nor powers,nor height nor depth, nor anything else in all creation, will be able to separate us from the love of God in Christ Jesus our Lord.

TRUST AND BELIEVE

When are you going to believe I have the ability
to bring into your life all the necessary tools
needed to fulfill My desires for you?

You work so hard and this need not be.

Trust that I will bring all things to you in due season.

I will not ask you to do more
than what I have prepared you for.

Please don't minister in your own strength,
believing you need to prove yourself to Me.
You will burn out and dry up.

As your needs arise, seek My face and
you will receive My strength, direction and provision.

It grieves My heart, when you think you have to earn
what I freely want to give you. (Philippians 4:19)

Come to Me for all your needs.
My store house is overflowing.

I own everything that has any real value.

Do not be afraid of receiving
all that I have in store for you.

Oh, how good and joyous your life will be,
when you start truly believing I want to provide for you.

So many promises will be revealed to you
as you start to accept Me as your loving Father.
(Colossians 1:26)
cc

WHAT DO YOU FEED ON?

*So many times I have sent you
My goodness and you have turned it away.*

*You must find your self-worth in Me.
Not in the world around you.*

*You are like a child who refuses to eat her vegetables.
The child needs the nourishment from the vegetables.
You need the nourishment from My love.*

*Do not be afraid of tasting Me
in a different way than you have known.
Please don't limit Me as My people of old did.
Let Me come to you in a new way.*

*Allow My Holy Spirit to reign in your life,
with full power and might.*

*My people need to realize the power that is waiting for them,
if they would just believe long enough to take a bite.*

*So many of My people fill up on what satan's kingdom has to
offer. They allow satan to fatten them up with pride,
greed, lust, jealousy and most of all misery and loneliness.*

*Many are full of themselves, but starving because they have
not allowed My Spirit to fill them.*

*When will they realize that the junk food of this world
is killing them spiritually?*

When will they realize, I Am the food they refuse to eat?

*My love is the only food that can fill a soul,
so completely that one will not desire
soulish food again.*

Many of My people are starving because they feed themselves
on the junk of this world
and not from the life of My Son.

Cleanse yourself from what you have fed on in the past.

Do not let people, places or the material world fill you.
As you will still be empty and lifeless.

Oh, come to Me this day.
I will give you health not sickness and
I will feed you well each day.

My love will shine forth from you.
You will be able to feed others
from the goodness and mercy I have fed you.
cc

John 6:35

Jesus said to them, "I am the bread of life; whoever comes to me shall not hunger, and whoever believes in me shall never thirst.

John 6:51-56

I Am the living bread that came down from heaven. If anyone eats of this bread, he will live forever. And the bread that I will give for the life of the world is my flesh." The Jews then disputed among themselves, saying, "How can this man give us his flesh to eat?" So Jesus said to them, "Truly, truly, I say to you, unless you eat the flesh of the Son of Man and drink his blood, you have no life in you. Whoever feeds on My flesh and drinks My blood has eternal life and I will raise him up on the last day. For My flesh is true food, and My blood is true drink. Whoever feeds on My flesh and drinks My blood abides in Me, and I in him.

Wealth

True wealth cannot be bought, sold or earned.
True wealth is found only through Me and My Kingdom.

My people need to realize,
material wealth is just a cheap imitation,
used to satisfy mans need to feel important and worthy.

Nothing a person has here on Earth, is truly his or hers.
It all belongs to Me.   No one can truly possess money,
without being greatly held responsible. All things in this
world are on loan to My people.

Do not become envious of those who have material wealth,
the price on the loan is great.

You must realize that anything that can be owned or bought
in this world has no lasting value to Me or to you.

A day is coming when I will return and ask all My people,
unsaved and saved, to give an account for what they did
(or didn't do) with all that I entrusted them with.
It doesn't matter how much or little you had.
What matters is what you did with it.

Your gifts and talents are the same way.
But in these, I will look at how many times
you took the glory instead of giving it to Me.
Whatever part you took credit for will be burned up.
Self cannot be glorified, only I can.

There will be so much heartache,
the day I judge My people's lives.

My people have been blind
to the evil ways and motives of their heart.

MOST of My people do not understand who they are in Me.
They believe their worth
is found in the wealth of this world
and not in the fact that I created them.

Your worth is not in what you have, where you can go or
in what you can accomplish.

Many people believe that their life has no value because they
do not have a lot of money.

I Am your provider, not money.

When a person believes they have no value,
they are not free to use all that I have given them,
because it is buried in doubt.

Please, let Me dig out and uncover the jewel that you are.

I have given you much and I will expect much from you.

My desires for your life will not be that hard to accomplish,
if you allow Me to do the work and receive the credit.
My love for you is great and My joy in you is everlasting.
cc

Matthew 6:19-21 & 24

"Do not lay up for yourselves treasures on earth, where moth
and rust destroy and where thieves breaks in and steal, but lay
up for yourselves treasures in heaven, where neither moth nor
rust destroys and where thieves do not break in and steal."

"For where your treasure is, there your heart will be also."

"No one can serve two masters, for either he will hate the one
and love the other, or he will be devoted to the one and despise
the other. You cannot serve God and money."

REMOVE THE BLINDERS

*I Am pleased when you come into My chambers, but there is a
cost of self each time you enter in.*

*The closer you get to My heart,
the more you can see what's really in your heart.
The more you see, the more you will realize that your motives
are not as pure as you thought they were.*

*How can the lost see that My Kingdom is different when My
children are still living in satan's kingdom?*

Stop believing that "to be somebody" you must earn it.

MY child, YOU ARE because I AM.

*Do not compare yourselves with the success of this world.
It is not success at all.*

*Success is found in one who completely gives his life to Me.
Success is being free to love, give and receive.*

*Do not see as the world sees.
Do not see at all if it's not by My spirit.*

*Do not feed yourself on the material things
of this world any longer.*

You must see that real wealth cannot be bought or earned.

True wealth is Eternal life in My kingdom.

It is the greatest inheritance a man can ever possess.

*It is freely given because My Son paid the price for anyone
who will receive Him and the sacrifice of His life.*

My heart continually breaks for the lost.

*Oh, how I have longed for thousands of years
to have My family complete.*

*When are My people going to take
My promises and Word seriously?*

*When will My children,
focus on My desires instead of their own?
My people have been so driven by their own want.
And not by My desires.*

*How it grieves My heart
to see My children starving.
They are starving to death while others are building up
satan's kingdom with money and knowledge that is intended
to feed My children physically and spiritually.*

*There are many who have a great abundance of riches tied up
for their own personal use.*

*Pray..... that My people will use their talents and finances for
My Glory instead of their own.*

*Pray for people to be released from the lustful
and greedy spirits that have been blinding mankind.*

*Cry out for My Son's mercy to fall upon those addicted to
pornography, gambling and drugs.
So they can be freed from these bondages.
(Matthew 9:12-13)*

*Claim the use of that money to be used for My children's
needs. Use the power I have given you.*

You must also pray that your blinders will be removed.

My people need to stop wanting this world
and start wanting Me.
Yes, I want you to prosper, but be satisfied at all times.
My people have been so selfish...
More clothes, more cars, more houses.

Can you not see these things are just temporal?
They have no real value in My eternal Kingdom.

My Children, let Me use what I have given you.

Nothing I give you is for you only.
You are to give it back to Me so that I can multiply it.

I want you to be able to freely give without fear.

It is time My child, to grow up
into the knowledge of who you are in Me.
Not only must you believe it, you must start walking in it.
cc

Titus 3:3-7

For we ourselves were once foolish, disobedient, led astray, slaves to various passions and pleasures, passing our days in malice and envy, hated by others and hating one another. But when the goodness and loving kindness of God our Savior appeared, He saved us, not because of works done by us in righteousness, but according to his own mercy, by the washing of regeneration and renewal of the Holy Spirit, whom he poured out on us richly through Jesus Christ our Savior, so that being justified by His grace we might become heirs according to the hope of eternal life.

I John 2:15-17

Do not love the world or the things in the world. If anyone loves the world, the love of the Father is not in him. For all that is in the world--the desires of the flesh and the desires of the eyes and pride in possessions--is not from the Father but is from the world. And the world is passing away along with its desires, but whoever does the will of God abides forever.

LET GO OF YOUR WORLD

My Child,
I have not asked you to give up the things that please you.
I Am asking you not to desire them more than Me.

Can you not see I want you to have happiness in all things?
But first, you must realize that it is within Me
that your true happiness is found.

I cannot have you searching in the world
to find My Kingdom. I Am the gate keeper.
Come to Me and I will hand you the keys to unlock all the
treasures found beyond the gates of this world.

Do not be afraid to step out of your comfort zone.
(Matthew 14:29-33)

You must trust that I can provide,
guide and lead you into The Kingdom.

Your false beliefs are the only thing holding you back from
receiving all that I have for you. Your mind has been so
narrowed by the way of this world and the words of man.
You must let go of what you think is reality.
Let Me show you what is real.

It is time for you to live in My Kingdom here on earth.
My ways are not your ways.
My will has not been your will. (Isaiah 55:6-9)

When will you realize that your flesh is no more than your
will and desires? Do not blame your enemies for what you
have allowed into your heart.
Come to Me and trade in your will for Mine.

Will I always have to compete
with your world for your attention?
When no one seems to notice your labors,

My Kingdom does.

When you feel overwhelmed, lean on Me.

*When you realize that your desires are not Mine,
hand to Me your disappointments.*

*When your will doesn't want to follow Mine, you must bring
your emotions and desires under My Command.*

*Do not let rebellion be your ruler.
(Ephesians 2:1-10)*

*Share with Me your deepest desires and thoughts,
Do not hide anything from Me.*

I do not want you to think without Me.

*Bring Me into your thoughts
so that I can speak Truth to you.*

*My thoughts and desires for you are much greater
than your mind can currently handle. (Ephesians 3:20)*

*Do not become upset when I lead you in a different direction
than the way you wanted to go.*

*At this point, you are not capable of choosing what's best,
because your mind is still filled with the limitations of man.*

*There will be many decisions, I will leave up to you to make,
but do not become independent and
assume you know My will for your life.*

*It is My desire to be deeply involved in everything you do.
Please don't leave Me behind while you play in your world.*

cc

LET ME UNVEIL YOUR EYES

*Many are looking for happiness in this world. The truth is,
I Am the only source of true lasting happiness.*

*I made you for My pleasure.
So, when you choose to please only yourself,
You will feel emptier than before.*

*Don't hide behind denial,
as I expose the sins of your heart.*

*Humble yourself, admit your faults and
your need to be saved from your own wickedness.*

*It's only when you realize that you have left My side,
that you can repent and turn towards Me again.*

*Why do you judge those who are still blinded by darkness?
Who has opened your eyes to see their sin?
Has it been your pride? As I remove the darkness from your
heart you will see with compassion not judgment.
(1 John 2:9-11)*

*I Am the only One to judge the heart of man.
Do you really believe that I would walk away from those who
need to be redeemed? I died for all.*

*Do you not realize that My people
are a part of My inheritance?
(Ephesians 1:18)*

*The veil has been lifted so those who want to see will see.
(2 Corinthians 3:14-18)*

*Why do you choose to stay alienated from Me? Do you not
realize there is more in Me than you presently have?*

> *As My people repent and turn*
> *from serving their own fleshly desires,*
> *I will satisfy their soul with the fullness of Me.*
>
> *When My Church is doing what I created it for,*
> *All creation will be set free to become One with Me.*
>
> cc

Romans 8:14-23

For all who are led by the Spirit of God are sons of God. For you did not receive the spirit of slavery to fall back into fear, but you have received the Spirit of adoption as sons, by whom we cry, "Abba! Father!"

The Spirit himself bears witness with our spirit that we are children of God, and if children, then heirs--heirs of God and fellow heirs with Christ, provided we suffer with him in order that we may also be glorified with him.

For I consider that the sufferings of this present time are not worth comparing with the glory that is to be revealed to us. For the creation waits with eager longing for the revealing of the sons of God. For the creation was subjected to futility, not willingly, but because of him who subjected it, in hope that the creation itself will be set free from its bondage to corruption and obtain the freedom of the glory of the children of God.

For we know that the whole creation has been groaning together in the pains of childbirth until now. And not only the creation, but we ourselves, who have the firstfruits of the Spirit, groan inwardly as we wait eagerly for adoption as sons, the redemption of our bodies.

MY BRIDE

I have waited so long, My bride,
for the day you would not run out on Me.

Tell Me today that you won't run again.

Give Me the commitment of your heart and life.

Do not let time come between Us.

Do not become impatient and go your own way.
Do not let this world lure you from My arms again.

How My heart ached each time I dressed to meet you,
My bride. But was left standing at the altar wondering why
I have to wait so long for you to truly commit to Me.
To love Me more than you love your independence.

Come and be with Me now and for all eternity.

Do not look at the world around you for My coming.
Look into your heart to see if I Am there.

It is through My people that I will be known in this world.

The people who will allow Me to live in their lives now,
will experience all of who I Am.

Do not wait to see Me in another.
let others see Me in you.

When you, My bride, will love Me more
than anything this world has to offer,
We will be One as My Father and I are One.
Then the wedding feast will take place.
(Revelation 19:7-9)
cc

Volume V

WHO YOU ARE IN ME

My people, you do not yet understand who you are in Me.

*How many times you have fed yourself
with the bitter words of man.*

*Oh, how you have allowed the words of man to mean more
than the words I have spoken. You have placed your worth
in the approval and opinions of man.*

*Do not be tempted any longer, to let the words of man feed
you... Your true worth cannot be measured or judged
by the mere mortal words of man.*

*Decide this day whom you are going to serve.
The opinions of man or Me?*

*Stop believing that your worth
can be earned or taken away.*

*Do not hide behind the words and deeds,
that make you feel worthy.*

I will soon strip them away from you and leave you bare.

*You must find your worth in Me and Me alone.
Only when you do this
can you be free from the words of man.*

*When you believe that you can do more,
to be more worthy, you are deceiving yourself.*

*If you allow the compliments of man to feed your ego
then you will also let the criticism of man
steal away "your" worth.*

You are worthy because I chose to create you.
You are worthy because I Am a part of you.

You are worthy because you are My child
and made in My image.

You are worthy because you're My Son's beloved.

You are worthy because I Am worthy.
cc

Genesis 1:26

Then God said, "Let Us make man in Our image, after Our likeness. And let them have dominion over the fish of the sea and over the birds of the heavens and over the livestock and over all the earth and over every creeping thing that creeps on the earth."

Galatians 3:26-29

for in Christ Jesus you are all sons of God, through faith. For as many of you as were baptized into Christ have put on Christ. There is neither Jew nor Greek, there is neither slave nor free, there is no male and female, for you are all one in Christ Jesus. There is neither Jew nor Greek, there is neither slave nor free, there is no male and female, for you are all one in Christ Jesus. And if you are Christ's, then you are Abraham's offspring, heirs according to promise.

1 Peter 2:9

But you are a chosen race, a royal priesthood, a holy nation, a people for His own possession, that you may proclaim the excellencies of Him who called you out of darkness into His marvelous light.

LIVING TEMPLE

Why won't you let Me share all My thoughts with you?
Ask yourself, why you choose to selectively hear Me?
It is My desire for you to hear Me clearly all the time,
not just when the world around you is silent.

Humble yourself enough to take My guidance.
Do not be fooled by believing, that in yourself
you possess wisdom apart from Me.

You do not know what is truly in the depths of your heart...
Are you willing to let Me search out your heart completely?
So I can reveal to you the darkness
that is still holding you captive.

Do you realize, I Am the only One
who can bring light into the areas of your soul
that have been darkened by fear and rejection?

I want to remove the darkness and despair,
but won't, until you realize your part and forgive
those who helped put the darkness of distrust there.

I Am not afraid of the darkness in your heart.
Why are you?
I Am big enough, strong enough and love you enough
to see you through the areas of hurt
that you have caused and the hurt that has come to you.

When, My child, are you going to trust
that I really love you enough to stay by your side forever?

The condition of your heart and the sins of your flesh
do not remove My love from you one bit.
It was sealed on the cross.

Let Me share your heart with you.
Let My light of love shine through your areas of darkness.

How can your soul be free
to laugh, play and be One with Me,
when you keep yourself
bound with heartache, worry and fear?

My child, I want you to be free from your past.
I want you to be free from the ways of this world
and the temptations in it.

Allow My kingdom to come to you here on Earth,
so you may know the joy you can have in Me.

You will never find the joy and release you need
"mentally" living in this world.

Your mind cannot be focused on the problems of this world.
You must let Me renew your mind and heart
with My truth and love. (Colossians 3:1-4)

I will not allow the sorrow of this world
to be buried in you, My living temple.
(1 Corinthians 3:16)
cc

Psalms 51:10
Create in me a clean heart, O God, and renew a right spirit within me. Cast me not away from your presence, and take not your Holy Spirit from me.

John 10:10
The thief comes only to steal and kill and destroy. I came that they may have life and have it abundantly.

Romans 14:17
For the kingdom of God is not a matter of eating and drinking but of righteousness and peace and joy in the Holy Spirit.

*H*EARING *M*Y *V*OICE

When you hear My voice it is because you believe you can.

*The only time you cannot hear Me, is when your own
thoughts are talking louder than My voice.*

Silence the thoughts of your mind.

*Take each thought that speaks against Me, under control.
(2 Corinthians 10:3-6)*

*Do not let your mind be swept away from Me.
Do not let hours go by without hearing Me.*

I Am forever speaking and waiting for you to respond.

*Do not become discouraged during this battle time.
It will take time to bring your
whole mind under sub-mission to Me.*

*Ask Me for help.
I have the ability to calm your thoughts: voices of worry,
doubt and fear. At this point these voices are your biggest
and strongest enemies. But I Am much stronger.*

*Yield your thoughts to Me continually.
Stop trying to battle them alone.*

*I Am the One who gives My people a sound mind.
A mind in peace and unity with Mine.
(2 Timothy 1:7)*

The battle for your mind will be won for My Glory.

*Soon no thought will hold your mind
from hearing My truth.*

No thought will be able to hold you in bondage.
Words not spoken from My Spirit
will fall to the ground and die.

Your mind will no longer be able to entertain
words that are not true.

No longer will your mind be as a whirlwind,
tossed to and fro by the opinions and beliefs of man.

You will be able to pause and hear Me at all times.

Choose this day not to follow your thoughts
or the thoughts of man.

Follow and listen for Mine instead.
cc

2 Corinthians 10:3-6

For though we walk in the flesh, we are not waging war according to the flesh. For the weapons of our warfare are not of the flesh but have divine power to destroy strongholds. We destroy arguments and every lofty opinion raised against the knowledge of God, and take every thought captive to obey Christ,

2 Timothy 1:7

For God gave us a spirit not of fear but of power and love and self-control.

Rely On Me

My child, I see your progress. Do you?

*Please don't become discouraged, as you do not yet realize
the eternal impact you're making for My Kingdom.
I see all that you do even when the world doesn't.*

*You will do even greater works in these coming months.
Do not fear the changes I will be taking you through.*

*Trust Me, knowing that I have a plan for you.
Listen more and you will hear more.*

Do not be tempted to feel lonely. I Am by your side.

*I have so much I wish to share with you.
So many wounds I want to heal.
My compassion for you is unending.*

Rely more on Me and not on this world.

*You have labored so. Rest My child. Rest in Me.
Knowing that I love you and I Am very proud of you!*

*I Am pleased with your devotion to Me.
You must realize that your value is in Me
and not what you can do for Me, or My people.*

*Do not carry guilt for the things of the past. Again I say
"Rest, let Me share with you the joy you bring Me."*

*When you can't hear Me, feel Me.
When you can't feel My presence then speak to Me.
When you run out of words to say, then rest in Me.
Knowing that I can see your heart for Me.
I truly do love you.....*
cc

COME TO ME, NOT MAN

*So many times you have opened your heart
to hear the opinions of man.
Do you not realize, that unless it came from Me,
it has no eternal value?*

*Oh, how you have allowed your heart and mind to be
tormented by the words of man.
Do not allow this any longer.*

*Do not eat for food, the words of man.
You are to live by My words alone...*

*Do you not realize that satan can and will try to speak to you
through people?*

*You must stop going to people for the answers you seek.
I Am the one you should seek.*

*I, more than anyone, want to see you in perfect health and
peace. Do you not realize, the only way this
can be accomplished is through Me?*

*Oh, how you have labored in vain!
Come to Me, so I can speak words of wisdom and comfort.
Please, realize that I know what is best for you,
in any given situation.*

*Do not hide your face from Me.
Do not be afraid of what I will say.*

*My words will bring life to your day
and death to your sorrows.*

*I will not "beat you up" with My holiness.
My child, have you forgotten,*

I Am the one to bring you into holiness?
I do not use guilt to manipulate My children to obey Me.

My ways are much higher.

By My breath, life was given to man.
How much more life is given by My spoken word?

I Am well pleased with your progress in Me.
Do not measure or compare your growth.

Do not become prideful, believing that your growth
makes you better than another.
Your growth enables Me to be glorified, not you.

Learn to listen to Me, not man.

Man can deceive, I will not.
Man will puff you up, I will humble you.
Man can lead you away from My will, I know My will.
Man's words can condemn you, Mine will set you free.
(2 Timothy 3:1-5)

Once again, come to Me and not Man.
cc

Jeremiah 29:11-13

For I know the plans I have for you, declares the LORD, plans for welfare and not for evil, to give you a future and a hope. Then you will call upon Me and come and pray to Me, and I will hear you. You will seek Me and find Me, when you seek Me with all your heart.

Colossians 1:6-7

for in Him were all things created, in the heavens and upon the earth, things visible and things invisible, whether thrones or dominions or principalities or powers; all things have been created through Him, and unto Him; And He is before all things, and in Him all things hold together.

ONE IN SPIRIT

You must learn to turn over every thought to Me.
Do not think only to yourself.
Think to Me. Which means talk to Me instead of yourself.

Do not have a thought without Me.
Direct all of your thoughts into a conversation with Me.

Abide in Me. Turn to Me continually, not yourself.
Give to Me the thoughts of your mind.
Let your mind become One with Mine.

Learn to notice when your mind goes astray.
Do not let YOUR thoughts run away from ME any longer.
(2 Corinthians 10:3-6)

Yield your whole mind to Me.
In return, I will fill it with My thoughts,
which are full of life and not despair.

Do not let your own beliefs wage war against
My truth any longer.

My child, your mind is daily being taken over,
one negative thought at a time.

You have allowed your mind to feed on:
fears - worries - anxieties - jealousy - doubt and anger.
Are these My thoughts, or yours?

My child, I know you hunger and thirst for real peace and
rest. You will never find it if you continue to listen to your
own knowledge (thoughts) instead of Mine.

Do not let your mind rule
you with thoughts that are not of Me.

Quit allowing your mind to tell you that We are separate.
In My Kingdom, there has been no separation
since My Son cleansed the world of sin.
The veil was torn between the two worlds.
(Hebrews 10:19-20)

The very second you asked My Son into your life,
HE began to LIVE IN YOU. He will never leave you.
(Galatians 2:20)

Do you not know, as one of My children,
you ALSO have the right and privilege
of being in My presence continually?

The only thing that keeps Us from being One in Spirit
throughout the day, is your mind
being allowed to have separate thoughts.

Even when you do not feel My presence, or hear My voice,
I Am still One with you...   Will you become One with Me?

Are you willing to let go of your separate world
of thoughts and desires?
cc

John 5:19

So Jesus said to them, "Truly, truly, I say to you, the Son can do nothing of his own accord, but only what he sees the Father doing. For whatever the Father does, that the Son does like-wise.

John 17:21-23

That they may all be one, just as You, Father, are in Me, and I in You, that they also may be in Us, so that the world may believe that You have sent Me. The glory that you have given Me, I have given to them, that they may be one even as We are One, I in them and You in Me, that they may become perfectly One, so that the world may know that You sent Me and loved them even as You loved Me.

*H*OLINESS

Your heart has been so restless.

Come to Me for the rest you so desperately need.

You struggle so with the ways of this world.
Let go of this world and come into Mine.

Do not keep one foot in and one foot out.

When you find yourself lost in this world,
cry out to Me and I will bring you back unto Me.

Do not fear that I will not hear you.
My ears are tuned to each of My children's voices.

I will not be angry but I will rejoice
that you realized you had left Me.

Do not let these words fall upon deaf ears.
Truly believe that I want you to be by My side.

The more your thoughts are with Me,
the more you will not want to be of this world.

My Son, Jesus, lived on Earth, but His heart, mind and soul
lived for Me, with Me and in Me.

You too, My child, will come to this place of maturity.
Be patient. I Am the potter, not you.
(Romans 8:29-30)

Come; let Me show you the cracks in your life
that need to be filled in with forgiveness, strength and love.

My child, you need to completely understand,
by yourself you can do nothing to become Holy.

You must acknowledge My Son,
as the only One, who is Holy enough
to take away your sins.

It's through His Holiness that you are made righteous.

You must realize that your part is to Repent (turn away) from
the sin, admit that you have sinned
and then ask for forgiveness.

You will never be free to grow in Me,
without wanting glory or recognition for your growth
unless you understand, it is not by your works but by Mine.

Let Me work through you...
cc

Matthew 22:37

And he said to him, "You shall love the Lord your God with all your heart and with all your soul and with all your mind.

Romans 5:17

For if, because of one man's trespass, death reigned through that one man, much more will those who receive the abundance of grace and the free gift of righteousness reign in life through the one man Jesus Christ.

1 John 1:19

If we confess our sins, He is faithful and just to forgive us our sins and to cleanse us from all unrighteousness.

Past the Veil of Accomplishments

Do not be troubled by the problems of this world.
(Colossians 3:1-2)

I have not called you to trust in the things this of world.
I have called you to live trusting in Me and My Kingdom.

Too many times, My child,
you have put your trust in the things of this world, and then
have fallen into disappointment.

When are you going to trust ME to meet all your needs?
(Proverbs 3:5)

My precious one, there is nothing in this world
that can truly satisfy you, like I can.

Open up to Me and My Kingdom for the needs you have.
Learn to trust Me with the things that disturb you daily.

Don't ever think, that even the smallest problem
is small enough for you to have to handle alone.

Each time you think you are strong enough to carry a burden
by yourself; you weaken your walk with Me.

Do you not yet understand?
I want you to share all of yourself with Me?

Each time you are weary,
it is because you have not used enough of My strength.

Do not hide your weaknesses from Me.
My child, I know everything about you and the problems you
choose to face alone.

I Am asking you today to stop hiding behind pride.
The false belief, that you should be stronger than you are
because of the many years you have served Me.

There will never be a day in your life
that I want you to feel strong enough to stand without Me.

It is through your willingness to grow and change
that My strength can be manifested in your new found
weaknesses. (2 Corinthians 12:9-10)

Do not look at your weaknesses as a defeat,
rather think of them as another opportunity
to grow in My strength. (2 Samuel 22:33-37)

My Bride, I Am preparing you for the day
when satan can no longer find a weakness in you.
Instead all he and others will find in you
is My Strength, Power and Glory.

Take joy in trusting Me with your
burdens, weaknesses and worry. (Matthew 11:28)

Have joy for the many things I have in store for you,
for the many places I will take you. (1 Corinthians 2:9)

Don't let anyone tell you that I won't use you
because of your weaknesses. I can use you more than the one
who is proud of his strengths.
(1 Peter 5:5-7)

When you hand Me your weaknesses and problems,
you allow Me to strengthen you with humility.

Please don't ever walk in shame before Me.
Instead walk with hope and belief in My ability
to bring about the changes needed in your life.
(Romans 8:1-2)

All you need to do is, yield to My Spirit
and believe the many promises I have given you.
Do not make walking with Me so hard,
that it is easier for you to walk with the world.
(Psalms 37:1-8)

Do not seek acceptance from the world,
when you "feel" unable to do enough for Me to accept you.

My child, I Am waiting with My arms of love opened wide,
to accept and forgive you,
no matter what you have done or not done.

Do not run from the only One who truly understands you.
Do not try to cover up your loneliness with success.

Come to Me.
I Am the only One who can fill
the longings you have deep inside.
Only My continual presence will satisfy you.

Step over - past the veil of accomplishments
and look at what is inside.

You will find Me and My Kingdom waiting to offer you true
acceptance, without any strings attached.
cc

2 Corinthians 12:9-10

But He said to me, "My grace is sufficient for you, for my power is made perfect in weakness." Therefore I will boast all the more gladly of my weaknesses, so that the power of Christ may rest upon me. For the sake of Christ, then, I am content with weaknesses, insults, hardships, persecutions, and calamities. For when I am weak, then I am strong.

THE QUIET VOICE OF ONE WHO LOVES YOU

My child, why do you act as if
I Am away on some far distant planet?

Can you not see Me in all things?

Learn to pause from the clamor of your daily life.
Look for Me and listen for My direction.

My voice can be heard softly and tenderly, to those who will
quiet their own thoughts, long enough to hear Mine.

Do not be discouraged if at first you don't hear.
It takes practice to calm your mind.

Can you hear a rain drop gently fall upon a pool of water
in the midst of a thunder storm? Than how do you expect to
hear My voice, when the stillness of your mind resembles the
cycles of a washing machine?

You continue to have so much turmoil in your life,
and this need not be so.

My written word says not to be anxious about anything.
Learn to rest your mind by giving Me all that troubles you.
(1 Peter 5:6-8)

The more you still your mind, the more you will hear Me.

I continually speak to you, sometimes even without words.
This, My child, is called the language of Love.

Learn to recognize My love in all things.
There are so many ways I want to show My love to you.
My child, words alone are not adequate enough
to express My love for you.
cc

LET ME LEAD YOU INTO THE IMPOSSIBLE

My people still rely so much upon themselves.
They labor and work much of the time without Me.

Do not be like My people of Moses
and refuse to acknowledge Me in all things.
Do not turn your back on Me,
the minute YOU think I have forgotten you.

Do not be afraid of intimacy with Me.
Do not become lazy
and choose not to climb up the mountain.
Do not rely on somebody else to hear Me for you.

Come to Me yourself, so that you can serve a living God.

My child, let Me be God to you.
Let Me show you the works of My Spirit.
Let Me show you the impossible.

But I caution you, My child, not to claim My works
as the works of your labor.

Do not become puffed up when I choose to work through you.
You must remember, it is for My Glory
and not your own.

You must not believe that your worth can be increased
because of the things I have you do for Me.

Your worth does not change before My eyes.
Your worth is complete in Me,
without the working of your hands.

You, My child, will not have to die in the wilderness,
if you believe in the impossible.

You will go forth to My promised land. The giants you have
to fight are the thoughts that hold you back.
Take every thought captive,
let not one escape and run wild.
(2 Corinthians 10:5)

Once you take possession of the giants
(your mind, will and emotions)
you will dwell in unity and Oneness with Me, forever.

Then you will truly see the impossible
because I will be doing it through you.
(Mark 10:27)
cc

Ephesians 2:1-10

And you were dead in the trespasses and sins in which you once walked, following the course of this world, following the prince of the power of the air, the spirit that is now at work in the sons of disobedience-- among whom we all once lived in the passions of our flesh, carrying out the desires of the body and the mind, and were by nature children of wrath, like the rest of mankind.

But God, being rich in mercy, because of the great love with which He loved us, even when we were dead in our trespasses, made us alive together with Christ--by grace you have been saved-- and raised us up with Him and seated us with Him in the heavenly places in Christ Jesus, so that in the coming ages He might show the immeasurable riches of His grace in kindness toward us in Christ Jesus.

For by grace you have been saved through faith. And this is not your own doing; it is the gift of God, not a result of works, so that no one may boast For we are His workmanship, created in Christ Jesus for good works, which God prepared before-hand, that we should walk in them.

WHO OR WHAT DO YOU TURN TO INSTEAD OF ME?

I Am looking for a people who will build faith and endurance,
from the things which are not seen.
Greater is the reward for those who believe and do not see!
(2 Corinthians 5:11)

In the wilderness, My people believed,
because of the things they saw Me do.
But the moment they could not see, they did not believe.

This is a time of building your faith.

When you turn away from Me in disbelief,
you are acting as Peter did when he denied Me.
He denied My presence and you deny My abilities.

Do not build your own idols
when you feel I Am not present.
Do not cling to them as if they were your god.
You must not put your security in the things of this world.

My child, do you really know what an idol is?
It's not just a piece of gold made into an "image".
It is anything you rely on or love more than Me.
An idol is who or what you turn to
when you don't turn to Me.
It is allowing something to take the place of Me.

What do you turn to?
A book... sleep... food... drugs or alcohol... television...
your own thoughts?

Who do you turn to instead of Me?
Church - your Pastor or Prophet - a close friend
the enemy? (1 Timothy 2:5)

Do not settle for an "image"
when you can have the real thing. (ME)

Will you choose to love Me
more than the people or things you currently rely on?

My child, I can break any addictions you may have and bring
you the comfort you have been seeking.

Are you willing to lay your idols down at My feet?
Are you willing to trust all to Me?

Are you willing to come to Me and Me alone.
To spend time getting to know Me?

I await your answer.
cc

Exodus 20:3-7

"You shall have no other gods before Me. "You shall not make for yourself a carved image, or any likeness of anything that is in heaven above, or that is in the earth beneath, or that is in the water under the earth. You shall not bow down to them or serve them, for I the LORD your God am a jealous God, visiting the iniquity of the fathers on the children to the third and the fourth generation of those who hate Me, but showing steadfast love to thousands of those who love Me and keep My commandments. "You shall not take the name of the LORD your God in vain, for the LORD will not hold him guiltless who takes His name in vain.

What is Holding You Captive?

What thoughts do you allow to beat you up?
What feelings do you let consume you?
My child, you must get past the point of allowing your
thoughts and feelings to control your daily life.

There will be many times you don't feel like doing something
that I have asked you to do. You must not let your feelings tell
you what you're going to do.

Feelings and emotions can deceive you.
You may feel one way, when the truth is another.

You may feel alone,
when the truth is I Am right by your side.

You may feel depressed,
when the truth is you were called to rejoice at all times.

You may feel that your circumstance is hopeless,
but I have called you to have hope.

You must not allow your emotions to be carried away by
negative feelings. You are to live by faith, not doubt.

When you start to feel overwhelmed, look towards Me,
not the problems you face. Do not indulge in thoughts and
feelings that will drag you down.

Adam and Eve knew only of life in Me until they ate of the
tree of self knowledge. They had not been introduced to
satan's world. They did not know of the deception that comes
from living in the world of self. I do not want you to live any
longer with the thoughts and beliefs that separate us.
The bondage of a self conscience that is no longer in union
with My Spirit. (John17:15-26)

Let your mind become One with Mine.
There is so much joy and peace in living with Me.

It was Eve's feelings of delight in the fruit of the tree of good
and evil that supported her decision to go against My spoken
word. She did not base her decision on truth (Genesis 3:6)

She based her decision on what she believed it would do for
her. She allowed satan to deceive her through reasoning with
her mind. She was caught up in self desire instead of pleasing
and obeying Me. Now Adam was not deceived. He knew the
truth and based his decision on fear. Not fear of Me, but fear
of what his life would be like without Eve.
He let his feelings for Eve
become more important to him than Me.

He chose to have a life with Eve instead of with Me.
He made Eve his idol. An idol that stopped his intimate walk
with Me. He turned to the door of sin instead of turning to
Me. I would have redeemed Eve right then if Adam would
have chosen Me.

Do not let your thoughts delight
in the things that are not of Me.
Do not let your actions be directed by your thoughts.
Do not eat from the tree of selfish desires.

Eat from My tree of Life and you shall be full of Life.

Do not let your mind feed on the thoughts of self pity and
despair or you will fall into bondage
to your own will and emotions.

You must begin to recognize what thoughts your mind is
feeding on throughout the day.
(2 Cornthians 10:4-6)
Are the thoughts you are chewing on, food from Me,
food from self or the enemy?

Who is feeding you? What are you feeding on?

Are you being nourished to fullness of Life? Or are you slowly starving to death from lack of faith and truth?

*Do not let your mind ponder on thoughts that are not true.
(Philippians 4:4-9)
You must learn how to fight off
the thoughts and feeling that are not of Me.*

Meditate on the miraculous ways I took care of those who loved Me. I will do the same for you, if you will truly believe and have faith in Me.

*Do not be a servant to the thoughts
that drive you away from My peace.
You are to be a servant to Me.*

Do not let your thoughts and feelings become the idol that separates you from becoming One with Me.

Do not stay in captivity any longer!

Turn to Me and not your own world of thoughts.

I LOVE YOU!!!
cc

2 Corinthians 10:3-6

For though we walk in the flesh, we do not war after the flesh:(For the weapons of our warfare are not carnal, but mighty through God to the pulling down of strong holds;) Casting down imaginations, and every high thing that exalteth itself against the knowledge of God, and bringing into captivity every thought to the obedience of Christ; And having a readiness to revenge all disobedience, when your obedience is fulfilled.

REAL LOVE

Will knowing Me make you feel more spiritual than others?
Will knowing Me make you wealthy?
Will knowing Me make you a great success?
Will knowing Me make you feel good?
What gain will you get from knowing Me?
Do you believe spiritual gifts will make you greater?

Many of My people who are in church
believe in Me, but don't know Me.
They have not digested My words completely,
nor correctly.

I will not make Myself known to My people, unless they ask
for Me and not for what they think they can get from Me.
I will only reveal the secrets of My Kingdom to those who are
ready to listen and obey My voice. (Luke 8:10-15)

My people have acted as their own god, for too long.

Even you, believe you know Me. I would say, "you have
known the things of Me, but not really know Me."
Those who really know Me completely trust Me.

What is more spiritual? Believing that you
know Me, or admitting that you don't?

I Am looking for a people, who will call on My name,
not just in a time of need,
but to spend time with Me and share their love with Me.

The only time most of My people will let Me into their lives is
when their role of playing god is failing.
I want a people, who will love Me
to the point of living for Me, and not themselves.

I laid My life down for you,
are you willing to do the same for Me?
So many, say they have laid down their life before Me.
But the truth is they pick it back up as soon as they feel a little
uncomfortable. Then say, "this must not be God" and again
choose to direct their own lives.

Do you really believe if you entrust your life to Me,
I will take care of you?

What will push your panic button, not to believe?
My child, your faith in Me is questionable.

Do you not know that it is I, who controls the winds of life?
I do not want any doubts left in your heart or mind.

Do you really believe in and Love Me?
Do you really believe that I love you?
Do you really know with what kind of Love?
Ponder on what real love means,
on the commitment and security that comes with real love.
(John 3:16-17) (1 Corinthians 13:4-13)

My love for you is real and everlasting.
Rest in this truth, until it becomes truth to you.
cc

Psalms 103:10-13

He does not deal with us according to our sins, nor repay us according to our iniquities.

For as high as the heavens are above the earth, so great is His steadfast love toward those who fear Him; as far as the east is from the west, so far does he remove our transgressions from us.

As a father shows compassion to his children, so the LORD shows compassion to those who fear Him.

For He knows our frame; He remembers that we are dust.

As for man, his days are like grass; he flourishes like flower of the field; for the wind passes over it, and it is gone, and its place knows it no more.

But the steadfast love of the LORD is from everlasting to everlasting on those who fear Him, and His righteousness to children's children, to those who keep His covenant and remember to do His commandments.

The LORD has established His throne in the heavens, and His kingdom rules over all.

Bless the LORD, O you His angels, you mighty ones who do His word, obeying the voice of His word!

Bless the LORD, all His hosts, His ministers, who do His will!

Bless the LORD, all His works, in all places of His dominion. Bless the LORD, O my soul!

CONCLUSION

I long for the fullness of Christ to be revealed in us.
To walk as Jesus did, listening to the Father throughout the day,
doing the Father's will and not our own.
All creation is groaning, waiting for us to grow up.
To realize who we are in Christ and to walk accordingly.

Romans 8:18-30

For I consider that the sufferings of this present time are not worth comparing with the glory that is to be revealed to us.

For the creation waits with eager longing for the revealing of the sons of God.

For the creation was subjected to futility, not willingly, but because of Him who subjected it, in hope that the creation itself will be set free from its bondage to corruption and obtain the freedom of the glory of the children of God.

For we know that the whole creation has been groaning together in the pains of childbirth until now. And not only the creation, but we ourselves, who have the firstfruits of the Spirit, groan inwardly as we wait eagerly for adoption as sons, the redemption of our bodies. For in this hope we were saved.

Now hope that is seen is not hope. For who hopes for what he sees?

But if we hope for what we do not see, we wait for it with patience. Likewise the Spirit helps us in our weakness. For we do not know what to pray for as we ought, but the Spirit himself intercedes for us with groanings too deep for words.

And He who searches hearts knows what is the mind of the Spirit, because the Spirit intercedes for the saints according to the will of God.

And we know that for those who love God all things work together for good, for those who are called according to His purpose.

For those whom He foreknew He also predestined to be conformed to the image of His Son, in order that He might be the firstborn among many brothers. And those whom He predestined He also called, and those whom He called He also justified, and those whom He justified He also glorified.

For additional copies or for the audiobook version,
please visit:

LessonsfromGod.org

Please let us know if this
book has touched your life.

For additional information
or to schedule a speaking engagement, contact:

Tim and Carla Cameron

ONE IN SPIRIT   Phone: 509.680.1338
MINISTRIES   Web: OneInSpirit.org

"Equipping the Body to Bring God Glory"

CPSIA information can be obtained at www.ICGtesting.com
Printed in the USA
BVOW08s0629131113

336177BV00001B/2/P